Chix
Can
Fix

NORMA VALLY

Chix Can Fix

100
Home-
Improvement
Projects
and True Tales
from the
Diva of
Do-It-Yourself

Viking Studio

VIKING STUDIO
Published by the Penguin Group
Penguin Group (USA) Inc., 375 Hudson Street, New York, New York 10014, U.S.A.
Penguin Group (Canada), 90 Eglinton Avenue East, Suite 700, Toronto, Ontario, Canada
M4P 2Y3 (a division of Pearson Penguin Canada Inc.)   ·   Penguin Books Ltd, 80 Strand,
London WC2R 0RL, England   ·   Penguin Ireland, 25 St. Stephen's Green, Dublin 2, Ireland
(a division of Penguin Books Ltd)   ·   Penguin Books Australia Ltd, 250 Camberwell Road,
Camberwell, Victoria 3124, Australia (a division of Pearson Australia Group Pty Ltd)   ·
Penguin Books India Pvt Ltd, 11 Community Centre, Panchsheel Park, New Delhi – 110 017,
India   ·   Penguin Group (NZ), Cnr Airborne and Rosedale Roads, Albany, Auckland
1310, New Zealand (a division of Pearson New Zealand Ltd)   ·   Penguin Books
(South Africa) (Pty) Ltd, 24 Sturdee Avenue, Rosebank, Johannesburg 2196, South Africa

Penguin Books Ltd, Registered Offices: 80 Strand, London WC2R 0RL, England

First published in 2006 by Viking Studio, a member of Penguin Group (USA) Inc.

10 9 8 7 6 5 4 3 2 1

Copyright © Norma Vally, 2006
All rights reserved

Drawings by Elmer and Elaine Suderino
Photographs by Jan Cobb
Creative consultant: Christopher Tirone

This book makes every effort to present accurate and reliable information. It is not a substitute
for professional electrical, plumbing, and other home building and repair services. If you are
not completely confident in proceeding with any of the repairs outlined in this book, you
should call a professional. Neither the author nor the publisher shall be liable or responsible
for any loss or damage allegedly arising from any information or suggestion in this book.

ISBN 0-14-200507-X

Printed in the United States of America
Set in Cochin and Trade Gothic
Designed by BTDNYC

IN LOVING MEMORY OF MY FATHER, PATRICK VALLY. *Mani d'oro,* FOREVER IN MY HEART, I HOPE YOU'RE PROUD OF YOUR LITTLE GIRL.

I'm extremely blessed to have been surrounded by so many wonderful people who have had a hand in making this book happen. Thank you, God.

To my mom, who puts the "grace" in "gracious," I am eternally grateful for her unconditional love and nourishment of my mind, body, and spirit.

To all of my cherished aunts, uncles, cousins, and friends who listened and supported my dreams in spite of my whining—thanks for the love! To cousin Sue, a huge merci for the inspiration. Special love and thanks to beautiful Aunt Rose-Marie, bro Roberto, Janne, Phyllis, Maria, Martha, Lucia, Carmela, Aldo, and cousin Sal.

To my literary agent, Maura Teitelbaum, for her unyielding determination and belief in *Chix Can Fix*, thank you. To my hosting agent, Mark Turner, thank you for being there for me from the very beginning. Thanks to my publicist, Amanda Leesburg, for her enthusiasm, vision, and perseverance. To Susanna Dalton, coach extraordinaire, great thanks for your guidance. Much appreciation to Oakley, especially Crishana Haynes, for keeping me covered with cool factor. Big time thanks to Shulz Industries and Bob Shulz Jr. for bringing the hottest tool belt on the planet to life.

Acknowledgments

Very special thanks to Aury Wallington for her awesome spirit, smarts, and humor.

To my creative consultant, Chris Tirone, for his tenacity, brains, and love—*grazie mille per tutto*.

For their brilliance, skills, and dedication, I'd like to thank the following people: Elaine Tirone, Elmer Suderio, and Wes Bailey.

For making it all so very beauteous I'd like to thank: my friend and makeup artist Cynthia Johnson, stylist Shoshanna Goldman, hair dresser Gregory D'Anna, and photographer Jan Cobb.

Thanks to Charles Baca and Exodus for the slammin' logo.

Great thanks to the entire team at Viking Studio, especially Lucia Watson.

A shout out to my *peeps* at Screaming Flea Production, Discovery Home Channel, and Discovery Channel Radio—thank you for giving *Toolbelt Diva* a place to play.

To my husband, Rick Medina, for his unwavering belief in me, back rubs, and inspiring me to dance naked to the sound of the printer, my deepest love and appreciation.

Contents

Chix
Can
Fix

Introduction

Thanksgiving Day, 1974. I was eight years old and we had just finished dinner. My entire family was there—my grandparents, aunts, uncles, cousins, parents, older brother, and me. What seemed like 142 people had already made it through three heaping courses of antipasto, soup, and pasta before we even got to the turkey! Three more courses followed that, topped off by a selection of Italian pastries that made the two-hour wait at the neighborhood bakery worth every minute. And finally pumpkin pie, to show just how Americanized my big Italian family had become.

Holidays had always involved mountains of food, but only now that I was old enough to clean did I realize that tons of food meant tons of dishes. And, as a girl, I was expected to help wash them after we were done eating, while the men—including my older brother—relaxed in the living room in front of the TV.

I grabbed the empty wineglasses off the table and carried them into the kitchen, where my mom and aunts were scurrying around, Brillo pads flying, stacking Tupperware with enough leftovers to last until Valentine's Day (and *no one* was getting out of the house without a bag of leftovers). I set the glasses down and was going back for more when, through the open doorway of the living room, I noticed my brother, Roberto, lying on the carpet watching TV and putting together a model car. I looked from him over to where my dad and uncles had passed out while watching the game, snoring so loudly they sounded like a symphony of wood chippers (Lord, could they snore with those Italian schnozzes of theirs). The women are working, the men are snoring.

Why does my brother get to watch TV while I have to dry the dishes? I had always known on some level that Roberto and I were treated differently because he was a boy and I was a girl. While I had never thought it was fair, what I realized then and what troubled me most was that the differences between us were more than just that he got to laze around while I had to work. As he sat there concentrating on his model car, I had what to my eight-year-old mind was an epiphany—there were things my brother knew how to do that I didn't simply because he was a boy.

My aunt Rose-Marie called to me from the kitchen to finish clearing the table, so I did as I was told, but while I was cleaning, my mind kept working around this epiphany. I couldn't understand it: My brother and I grew up in the same house, with the same parents, went to the same schools, yet he had access to knowledge and skills that I didn't.

How did he know how to fix a radio or take apart the lawn mower and put it back together? When did he learn to replace his bicycle chain every time it fell off? Were all the boys gathering in some no-girls-allowed clubhouse where they were coached by male elders on how to be mechanically inclined? Somehow my brother had learned, by the age of thirteen, to mount a twenty-foot CB antenna to our roof and ground it with a wire that he ran down the side of the house and secured into the dirt with a fork. Sure, when my parents pulled up to the house and found what looked like the top of the Empire State Building sitting on top of their house, they were royally pissed. But at the same time, I knew that my dad was secretly proud of my brother's ingenuity and courage for actually getting that thing up there.

I might not have understood why boys just seemed to know how to do things that girls didn't (and I still haven't quite figured it out), but I did know that anything my big brother could do, I could do, too. Little by little, I began to acquire those skills, and I eventually caught up. I didn't become a fix-it diva overnight. In the past thirty years, I've learned a lot about a broad range of construction and home-improvement skills. I've made plenty of mistakes along the way, but I never stopped trying, and I never gave up on the notion that I was fully capable of fixing anything I put my mind to, regardless of my gender. When my dad and uncles realized that I wanted to learn the same things they were teaching my brother and male cousins, they were surprised, but more than happy to teach me. And by working with them, I learned that gender doesn't matter—education does. I didn't realize it at the time, but on that Thanksgiving Day, almost thirty years ago, the idea for *Chix Can Fix* was born.

Chix Can Fix is your education. It's not going to take you thirty years to learn how to fix up your home, and you don't need to make the mistakes I did, because you have this book to guide you. I'm not ashamed to admit that I've fallen off a ladder or two, but you don't need to worry about falling—this book will keep you steady and confident.

My friend Susanna says, "If only I could figure out how to wire my surround sound, I wouldn't need a man around at all." To this brilliant, funny, talented, and successful woman, wiring her surround sound is the great enigma of life. Who wants to be waiting around for that guy who's been promising to hang those shelves you bought six months ago that are still sitting at the bottom of your closet collecting dust? I mean, we love men and all, but do we really want to put our lives on hold for that guy? Is this what is meant by being a lady-in-waiting? Well, those days are over. If a woman wants surround sound, she can have it. I'll show her how to do it herself. And I'll show you, too.

So come on. Pick up your screwdriver, put away your doubt, and let's get started.

Before You Begin:
Answering the What-Ifs

What if you're in the middle of a project and it all goes south? As they say, sh*t happens, and anyone who has ever tackled a home-improvement project knows this to be true. I don't care if you're a twenty-five-year construction veteran or a brand-new do-it-yourselfer. Parts don't fit, pipes break, measurements don't add up—you can't anticipate everything! Just know that when a problem arises, it isn't your fault, accept that it's the nature of the beast, and remember—the absolute best possible tool you can arm yourself with to handle any crisis is the right attitude.

I've developed a list of do's and don'ts—not necessarily in that order—so if you ever get caught up the ol' creek, you'll have a paddle.

DON'Ts

- Don't, out of frustration, chuck a freakin' tool at the wall—you'll only be setting yourself up for a wall repair.
- Don't run crying, "You were right! I can't do it myself!" to your father/boyfriend/husband. (That said, don't tell your father/boyfriend/husband he's the last person in the world you'd ever call on for help—just in case you end up needing a little backup.)
- Don't make a mountain out of a molehill. Come on, you're not performing open-heart surgery; you're replacing a washer.
- Don't panic. Dial 911 only if there's a real emergency—and an impenetrable toilet clog doesn't constitute a real emergency. If you've run into a problem you can't solve, calm down and call in a professional.

DO's

- Do familiarize yourself with all the tools, parts, and safety measures before getting started on your project.
- Do be patient with yourself. If Rome wasn't built in a day, your shelves may not be either.
- Do work methodically and neatly, so if you get stuck, you'll know exactly where you are in the project.
- Do step back and take a break if you hit a rough spot—sometimes that's all it takes to come up with a fresh solution.
- Do have the name and number of a professional handy in case you get in over your head.
- Do set yourself up for success by being informed about your project, equipped with the right tools, and prepared with a realistic budget and time frame for its completion.

Plumbing

My aunt *Rose-Marie,* God love her, is a true eccentric. She wears a ring on every finger and tells jokes that would make a truck driver blush, yet she goes to church at least three times a week. Call her Rose*mary* instead of Rose-Marie and risk getting the Sicilian look of death. It's 2005 and it's like she's still living in the Old Country, or at least back in the fifties. She's got rotary phones, plastic slipcovers on the couches, a freezer that you have to thaw out weekly, and a washing machine in the kitchen.

Rose-Marie won't travel outside Brooklyn for fear that she can't leave the house behind. My mom has been bugging her for years to come visit her in Las Vegas, but there's just no way—she's convinced the house would be gone by the time she got back. She also thinks that visiting anywhere an hour outside of New York City is like going to "the country," and she'll start speaking with a Southern drawl, imitating (in her own mind) the country folk—meanwhile she's gone all the way to the wilds of Hoboken, New Jersey.

My family's campaign to convince Aunt Rose-Marie that nothing would happen to her house if she left it for more than a few hours was dealt a serious blow last year. One evening when she came home late from novena night at church, she opened the door and let herself inside without turning on the lights. As she walked through the kitchen toward her bedroom, she simultaneously heard a *squoosh, squoosh* noise under her feet and felt something cold spraying her in the face.

She wondered, *What the hell is going on?* She fumbled for the kitchen light and found water jetting out from behind the washing machine. The flood that began in the kitchen had leaked into the hallway and down the walls to the basement. Alone in the house without a clue about how to stop the water, Aunt Rose-Marie tried cursing, then praying, and when neither of those worked, she decided to call her nephew Sal.

How do I describe Sal? He's the kind of guy you want to hug and shoot, both at the same time. He'll be there for you in an emergency no matter what time day or night, but while he's doing you a favor, he has the uncanny ability of finding your last nerve and dancing the tarantella on it until you either (a) tell him you will rip his balls off and throw them out the window or (b) vacate his presence completely. You'll hear him laughing about either one of your responses for days—that is, after all, why he acts that way.

So Aunt Rose-Marie calls Sal at midnight. I wasn't there, but to hear Sal tell it, it went something like this: "Sally! The whole f'in' house is under water! The f'in' washing machine is possessed! Do you see why I can't leave this house to go on f'in' vacation?!"

Sal says, "Aunt Ro, calm down and go shut off the water main." Now, Sal was one of the people who taught me everything I know about plumbing, and this was great advice. Unfortunately, my aunt's response was, "What the hell is a water main? Where the hell is it? And my sister wants me to go visit her in Las Vegas?! I'd come back and the house would be floating down Eighty-sixth Street!"

She was hysterical, so Sal told her again to calm down and he'd be right over. (That's why we love Sal.) Ten Our Fathers later, he showed up, went down to the basement, and shut off the main. That problem was solved, but the next half hour was spent trying to shut off Aunt Ro's personal waterworks—she was a crying, cursing mess. Then hours of cleanup ensued, and all the while she was swearing never to leave the house again for more than an hour at a time.

Clearly, the enormity of this mess could have been avoided if Aunt Rose-Marie had known where the water main was. (Better yet, it never would have happened if the water lines to her washer had been replaced with braided lines that don't burst, but we'll discuss that later.) Before the same thing happens to you, be prepared.

PLUMBING BASIX: UNDERSTANDING YOUR WATER SYSTEM

Labeling is just the beginning. In order to fix something, you need to have an understanding of how it works. That way you're not working blindly, in a void. Here's a basic overview of how plumbing works in your home. There are three systems: water-supply, drain-waste, and vent.

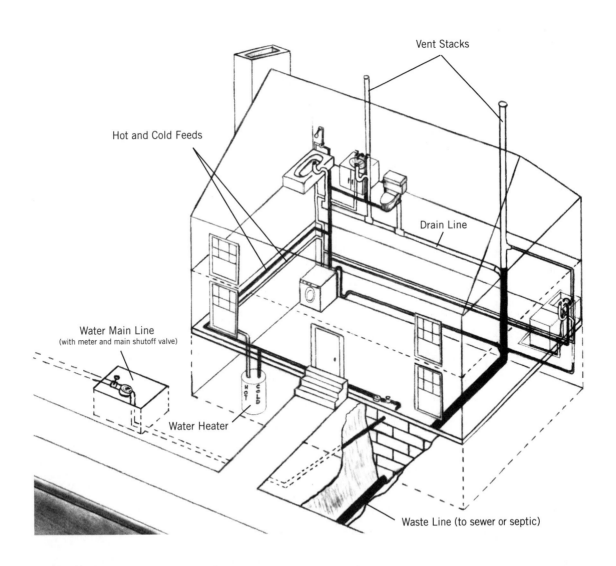

Vent Stacks

Hot and Cold Feeds

Drain Line

Water Main Line
(with meter and main shutoff valve)

Water Heater

Waste Line (to sewer or septic)

Water-Supply System

The water supply is carried into your home from a utility source or your own well via your water main. Once it enters the house, it passes through your water meter, then divides off to your various fixtures and appliances. Before reaching its destination, the cold water will sometimes pass through a softening or filtration system, while the hot water will pass through some type of heating system, like a hot-water tank.

Drain-Waste System

The used water (called "gray water") and waste go down your drain-waste system into your sewer main and are carried to the city sewer or your own septic tank. Each drain has a trap—either a P-trap or an S-trap (in older homes)—which is a bend in the drainpipe that always holds water and creates a barrier to block sewer gases from backing up into your home.

P-Trap

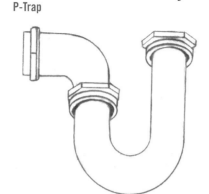

S-Trap

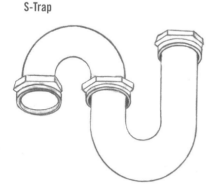

Vent System

The vent system exists for two reasons. First, if a drain-pipe and trap are empty, the vent carries noxious sewer gases up and out of the house, where they are released through pipes out of the roof. Second, the vent system creates downward pressure on water as it exits the drain system, allowing gravity to do its job. Without it, water would be trapped in the drain system, like when you hold your thumb over the top of a filled straw. The liquid won't flow out the bottom of the straw until you lift your thumb, creating a vent.

Drain-waste and vent systems are referred to as DWV because they are interconnected. DWV work together, in that each drainpipe is vented after the trap. The vent then leads to a main vent stack that exits up through the roof, and each drainpipe continues to a main soil stack that exits down through the sewer main.

Locate and Label Your Water Supply

If you're like most women I know, you can tell from fifty feet away if a bag is Prada, but when it comes to looking at a bunch of pipes and figuring which one is your supply line, you're at a complete loss. What is it about a designer label that makes us spend ten times more than we would for something sans label? I tried on a pair of black suede Sergio Rossi boots the other day, and it was love at first sight. They were a work of art. They brought me to tears. They cost $850 . . . ouch. Painful, but I could almost justify the cost, considering how they made my heart race, which was more than the last guy I went on a date with could do for me. But what about these shredded jeans or those synthetic handbags that are the price of a down payment on a car?

Okay, I understand that most women have been fashion victims at one time or another, but what I refuse to let us be is utility victims. This is where a few important labels can help you instead of hurt you. Do you know where your water main is? What about the shutoff valves for your bathroom and other water fixtures? If you want to take control of your home, the first thing you need to do is identify and label each of your utility sources. This section will explain the basics of your water system and reveal the truly important labels—the ones you attach to your water system so you know which pipe is which in the event of an emergency. (I'll also instruct you to do the same to your electic and gas systems later in the book.) This way, if there *is* an emergency, fashion or otherwise, you won't get caught with your pants down.

Locating Your Water Main

Water that goes where it shouldn't can cause a world of harm, and knowing how to quickly access your water main can spare your home from major damage. When minor leaks arise from a sink or toilet, you can just shut off the valve for the water supply to the fixture. But if you have a serious leak originating from a fixture that doesn't have a shut-off valve (or you can't find the valve) or if you just can't determine where the leak is coming from, you will have to *run,* not walk, to your main and shut it down. You'll also need to shut down the water in your home from the main if a fixture you want to repair doesn't have its own shutoff valve. Whatever the case may be, sleep better knowing that you won't nearly drown in your own kitchen, like my aunt Rose-Marie almost did, if you know where your water main is and you keep it clearly labeled.

In order to find your water main you'll have to do a little investigating. A water main is the pipe that runs your water supply from the utility source to your property and into your home. Since your water main will run through a water meter, first locate your water meter. This could be outside in the ground, attached to the side of the house, in the garage, or in the house (usually in colder climates). Once you locate the meter, look at the large pipe that runs through it—that's your water main.

Your main will have at least one shutoff valve. Typically, there will be a utility shutoff valve that will shut water down before it runs through the water meter and into your home. This utility shutoff will shut down all water sources inside and outside your home. If you are doing work on sprinklers or a hose bib, you will need to access this valve since it is

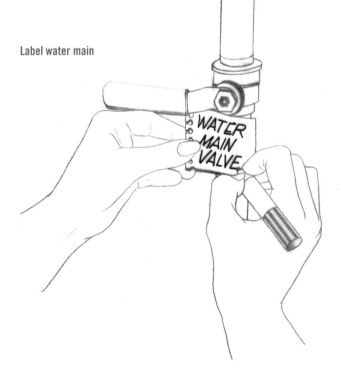

Label water main

the only way to turn off the water supply for the exterior of your property. You will probably need a wrench or a meter key to turn this valve to the "off" position. Label this valve and keep your wrench or meter key near it for quick access in case of an emergency.

If you have well water, there should be a shutoff valve at the source or along the water line before it enters your home or both—label them. If you live in an apartment, ask your maintenance person if you have a shutoff valve dedicated to just your apartment. Then ask to be shown where it is.

Often a home will have a second shutoff valve located along the water main that cuts off water just in the house. This shutoff valve will be positioned farther along the water main at a point after where the water has run through the water meter. It is usually in the garage or somewhere on the outside of the house. Label this water main valve so you know how to immediately shut down the water in your home.

TALKIN' 'BOUT TOILETS

You may never be on a toiletless construction site like I have been, but you can still save yourself from the bowl blues by knowing how to tackle a troublesome toilet.

Chix Chat:
When There's Nowhere to Go

They say that life is a bowl of cherries. But at two in the morning, when you're wrestling with a clogged toilet bowl, you will wish it was cherries you were dealing with. A toilet is something you can really take for granted— until you don't have one. I've had the distinct displeasure of being on job sites where the toilet has been taken out or there's no running water. You got that? NO TOILET, NO RUNNING WATER. A woman's worst nightmare. Out of dire necessity, I've

Toilet

Ballcock

Flush Handle Arm

Fill Tube

Ball Stop

Overflow Tube

Flush Valve

Hollow, perforated rim allows water to enter bowl from tank

Float Cup

Trap

Shutoff Valve

Johnny Ring (cutaway)

To sewer or septic tank

had to become extremely creative figuring out how to go to the bathroom in such ungodly conditions. I've mastered the art of squatting and peeing in a joint-compound bucket without falling in or splashing my boots—trust me, not easy tasks. I've mentally mapped every fast-food restaurant in Brooklyn with a clean bathroom, from Bensonhurst to Canarsie. I've acquired the world's largest collection of Dunkin' Donuts napkins, because they're kind of soft and large enough to do the trick when there's no toilet paper to be found (which is always the case at construction sites).

How to Get Your Tank on Empty

When performing a repair in your toilet's tank, you first have to shut down the water supply and drain the tank so you can get at the part you want to fix or replace.

TOOLS
- Large sponge
- Bucket

Toilet shutoff valve

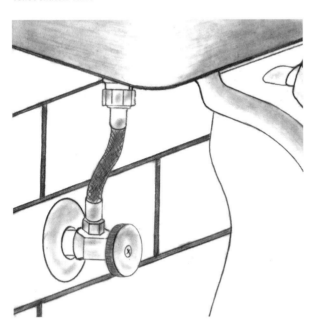

1. Shut off the water running to the tank by closing the shutoff valve by turning the handle clockwise. This valve is usually located in the lower corner behind the toilet. If you live in an older home, there may not be a shutoff valve to your toilet. In that case, shut off the water main. (If you don't know where your water main is go to "Locate and Label Your Water Supply" on page 13.)
2. Flush the toilet, emptying out as much water from the tank as possible.

3. Using a big fat sponge (the bigger the better), absorb the remaining water in the tank and squeeze it out into your bucket until the tank is dry.

Fixing a Noisy Toilet

Chix Chat:
Do I Need a Plumber or a Priest?

Being alone in my big old house can be pretty creepy sometimes. Steam pipes bang, wood creaks, wind blows through all the uninsulated nooks and crannies—it's like the soundtrack of *The Amityville Horror.*

But the rational part of my brain (the part that isn't telling me to hide under the covers) knows where all those noises come from and calms me down. That is, at least until the first time I heard the swoosh. *Swwwooooooosh. Swwwwooooooosh.* In the middle of the night, I wake up, not sure where the noise is coming from, not even positive I heard anything at all. *Swwwooooooosh.* No, I definitely hear something.

I feel like I'm eleven years old again, when I'd stay up late watching *Creature Features* (remember the hand that used to come out of the mud with six fingers *"Chiiiillller!"*) and then wouldn't be able to sleep all night.

But I'm not eleven, I'm an adult, and I need to find out what's making that noise. *Swooosh.* It's coming from the bathroom—something is alive in the bathroom! With trembling fingers I reach for the light . . . but there's nothing there. I'm about to go back to bed, when—*SWWWOOOOOOSH.* Great, it's the freakin' toilet bowl.

If *you* hear a *swoosh,* your bowl isn't possessed, nor is your dead uncle trying to contact you from the dead, either. That sound is the water running into the tank. Sometimes toilets make some freaky noises, and the most likely causes are a leaky stopper or the fact that the water level is too high. Lucky for you, both of these problems can be easily fixed, without consulting a plumber—or an exorcist!

Cleaning the Valve Seat

The swooshing sound you hear could be due to the toilet refilling itself because the tank stopper isn't sealing properly. To silence the swoosh, you'll need to correct the leaky seal between the valve seat and the tank stopper. So before you try anything else, scour the valve seat with steel wool. If it is pitted or has lime deposits, cleaning it may be all the fix you need to allow the stopper to again create a tight seal.

TOOLS
- Steel wool

1. First, empty the tank (see "How to Get Your Tank on Empty," page 16).
2. Scour the valve seat with steel wool until smooth.
3. Turn your water back on via the shutoff valve or the water main to refill the tank. Flush, wait for the tank to fill, and listen to the toilet to make sure it isn't still running.

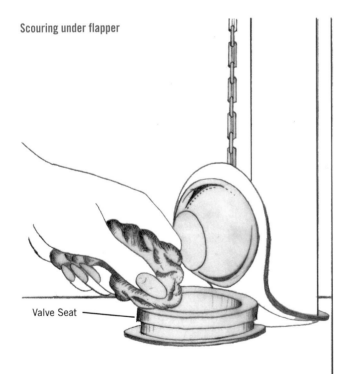

Scouring under flapper

Valve Seat

Replacing the Tank Stopper

If scouring the valve seat doesn't do the trick, you'll need to replace the tank stopper. There are two types of tank stoppers: ball stops and flappers. When the water leaks out and drops to a certain level, the inlet valve will open to let water come in and fill the tank up again.

TOOLS
- Your hands
- Replacement stopper

1. Empty your tank (see "How to Get Your Tank on Empty," page 16).

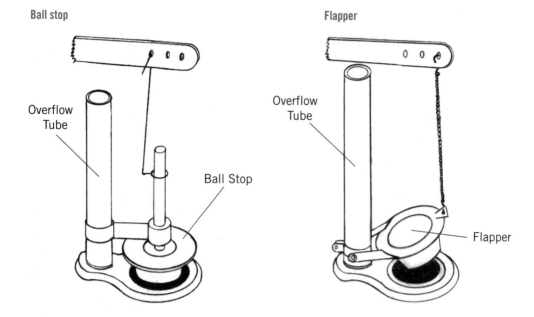

Ball stop

Overflow Tube

Ball Stop

Flapper

Overflow Tube

Flapper

2. Unhook the chain or unscrew the lift wire from the stopper, then pull the stopper off or over the overflow tube. If it turns your fingers black, that is because the rubber is worn out.

3. Take your used stopper to your local hardware or plumbing store and ask the salesperson to get you the *exact* part. If the store doesn't have your stopper, they may try to sell you another one that they claim is "universal." But don't be fooled—there's really no such thing. A universal stopper won't work correctly, and if it does, it won't last for very long. Go to another store and find the right stopper for your toilet.

4. Attach the stopper to the overflow tube.

5. Hook the chain or attach the lift wire to the new stopper.

6. Be sure to make any necessary adjustments to the length of the chain to ensure that the new stopper drops directly over the valve seat.

7. Turn your water back on via the shutoff valve or the water main to refill the tank. Flush, wait for the tank to fill, and listen to the toilet to make sure it isn't still running.

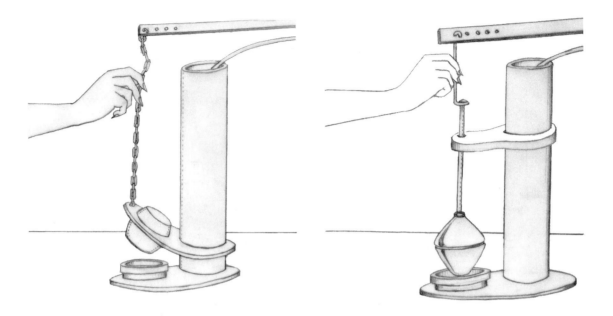

Unhooking chain   Unscrewing lift wire

Adjusting the Water Level in Your Tank

The water level in the tank should be approximately an inch lower than the overflow tube. If your tank's water level is too high, it will continually pour into the overflow tube, making a "running" sound. You'll need to adjust the water level so that it is lower than the overflow tube, but not so low that you have an inadequate volume of water for your flush.

After each flush, your toilet automatically determines the water level in the tank with a floater that triggers the water-inlet valve to shut once the water level reaches a certain height. Your toilet will have either a float ball or a float cup that performs this function. Look into your tank to see if your floater is a cup or a ball, and then follow the appropriate directions below.

TOOLS
- Screwdriver, flathead or Phillips (as needed)
- Replacement float ball

Float ball

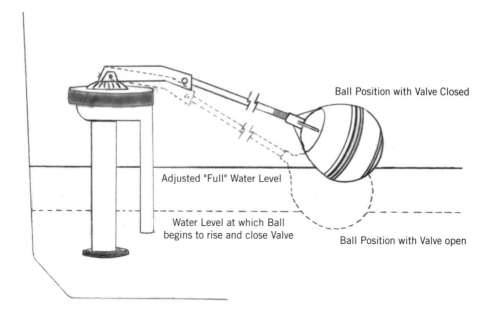

Ball Position with Valve Closed

Adjusted "Full" Water Level

Water Level at which Ball
begins to rise and close Valve

Ball Position with Valve open

TO ADJUST A FLOAT BALL

1. Check the ball to make sure it's not taking in water. If it's spongy, you'll need to replace it. To replace the ball, simply unscrew your old one from the float arm and take it to a hardware store to find a replacement. Then just screw on the new one.
2. If the ball that's already there looks fine, screw it in tighter, which creates a shorter distance between the float and the inlet valve and stops the inflow of water sooner.
3. Flush, wait for the tank to fill, and listen to the toilet to hear if it stops running.
4. If the toilet still runs, you should try adjusting the float arm. If the arm is made of metal, bend it downward, lowering the float, which will lower the water level and cause it to shut off the inlet valve sooner. Bend the arm upward for a higher water level. If there is an adjustment screw at the top of the float arm, turn this screw in either direction to raise or lower the arm. A plastic float arm cannot be bent and will have a screw for adjustments. Flush again and listen.

1. Squeeze the clip that attaches the float cup to the rod that triggers the inlet valve.
2. Slide the float down to lower the water level, or slide it up the arm to raise the water level. Flush and listen.

Whichever is the appropriate adjustment for your tank, the level must be approximately an inch lower than the overflow tube. Getting it there may take a couple of tries. Happily, either of these fixes should put an end to the *swoosh*. Now all you have to worry about is that spooky clanking sound coming from the attic. . . .

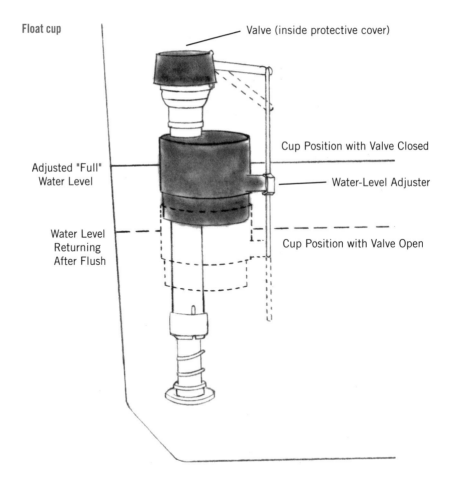

Float cup

Valve (inside protective cover)

Cup Position with Valve Closed

Adjusted "Full" Water Level

Water-Level Adjuster

Water Level Returning After Flush

Cup Position with Valve Open

Cool Tool:
Using a Hacksaw

The word "hacksaw" sounds like it should be in the title to a sequel of *Texas Chainsaw Massacre.* The name sounds intimidating but the tool itself is not. A hacksaw is a hand tool that is extremely useful and versatile. It is available in different shapes and sizes, with replaceable blades.

A minihacksaw with a pointed nose and fine-toothed blade is ideal for getting in tight spaces—like old rusty mounting bolts on your toilet base. Larger hacksaws are ideal for cutting metal or plastic pipes.

On a stable and raised work surface, hold the material to be cut in one hand (or put it in a vise) so the cutting point hangs over the edge of the work surface. Line up the blade at the top of the material and pull the blade firmly toward you, making a slit in the material. Be careful to keep the hand holding the material far away from the blade—the blade can bounce if you don't notch the material on your first pass and could cut your hand. The blade may "stick" in the material at first, making your sawing motion jerky, but stay with it—it will get easier the deeper into the material you go.

If you need to cut material that is attached to something, like bolts on a toilet, be cautious not to scratch the fixture surface. Carefully hold the blade parallel to the fixture, but perpendicular to what you're cutting and take short strokes if necessary to avoid hitting any delicate surface.

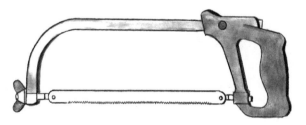

Shutoff valve

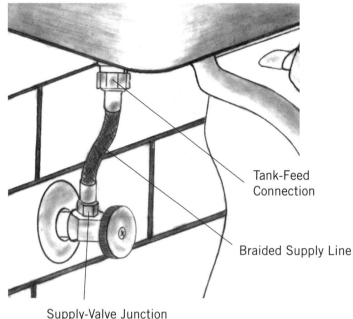

Tank-Feed
Connection

Braided Supply Line

Supply-Valve Junction

Repairing a Leaky Toilet

Ever find a trace of liquid pooled on the floor around your toilet? At
first you want to blame the last guy who used the bathroom for taking
such poor aim. Only . . . you haven't had a guy over in months (which
is a problem I can relate to and the subject for a different book!). So
where'd that liquid come from? *Could I have done that?* No, girl, it wasn't
you! The culprit is the toilet itself.

To stop the leak, you need to find out where the leak originates. There
are four possible sources:

- the water-supply line
- loose tank-mounting bolts
- the wax gasket (aka Johnny ring)
- cracked porcelain

Sorry to tell you this, but the only way to find the leak is to go down
on your hands and knees and get up close and personal with your toilet.

(Word to the wise: Clean your toilet and the surrounding floor thoroughly, dry them, then feel around for wet spots before you hunker down.) Unfortunately, if you see a crack in your bowl, you're screwed. Yeah, yeah, they sell products to repair porcelain cracks, but I'm not a believer. You have to replace your bowl. At this point I suggest calling in a professional.

But if the leak originates from a water-supply line, the tank-mounting bolts, or the wax gasket, fixing your toilet leak could be as easy as tightening a couple of nuts or bolts. If the leak can't be fixed by simple adjustments, you may have to replace some parts. Go through each of these fixes step-by-step and see if one of them applies to your drip.

The Supply-Line Fix
Use this fix if your toilet is dripping along the supply line.

TOOLS
- Adjustable wrench
- No-burst steel braided supply line (if applicable)

1. Look at the supply line to your toilet. If it's dripping from the supply-line connection at the tank, tighten the nut with an adjustable wrench. Do not overtighten—that will squash the washer completely, hindering it from creating a seal.
2. If it's dripping from the shutoff valve to the supply line, tighten that nut. Again, don't overtighten.

ATTACHING A NEW SUPPLY LINE
If your supply line is still dripping after you try tightening the nuts on the supply line and shutoff valve, you'll need to put in a new supply line. If the shutoff valve itself is leaking, replace that (see "Replacing a Shutoff Valve," page 76).

TOOLS
- Adjustable wrench

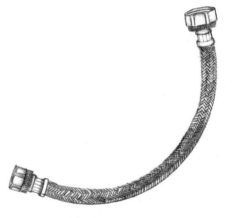

Braided line

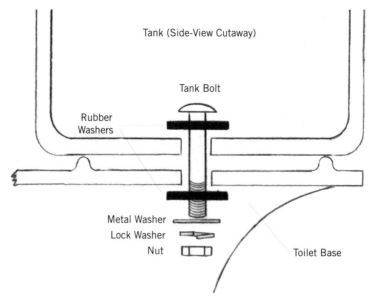

Tank-mounting bolts

Tank (Side-View Cutaway)

Tank Bolt

Rubber
Washers

Metal Washer
Lock Washer
Nut

Toilet Base

1. Empty your tank (see page 16).
2. Unscrew the old supply line at the shutoff valve and at the tank, using the adjustable wrench.
3. Replace the old line with a no-burst, braided line for toilets, being sure the replacement is long enough to span from the shutoff to the tank. (See "Replacing Flexible Water-Supply Lines," pages 73–74.) Again, don't overtighten.

The Tank Mounting-Bolt Fix
Use this fix if your toilet is dripping from the bottom of the tank, at the tank mounting bolts.

TOOLS
• Adjustable wrench or tongue-and-groove pliers
• Screwdriver, flathead or Phillips
• New bolts and washers (if applicable)

1. Empty the tank (see page 16).

2. Tighten the nuts by holding back the nuts outside of the tank with a wrench, and tightening the screws inside on the bottom of the tank with a screwdriver. Do not overtighten, or you risk cracking the porcelain.
3. If it still leaks, your washers are probably shot, so unscrew and remove the old bolts and washers, bring them to your plumbing-supply or hardware store, and replace them.

The Leaking Wax Gasket Fix

Use this fix if there is water seeping from the base.

If water is seeping out from under the base of the bowl, you need to replace your wax gasket (also known as a Johnny ring). This wax ring makes a seal between the porcelain toilet base and the flange that connects to the drainpipe. It keeps flushed water from leaking out of the toilet base and stops sewer gases from leaking into the house. FYI: If your bathroom has a persistent, *undesirable* smell (don't make me identify it!), you should try replacing the Johnny ring. This is a challenging project, so you will probably need a friend to help you.

TOOLS
- Adjustable wrench or tongue-and-groove pliers
- Hacksaw
- Scrap of carpet or cardboard
- Scraper
- New mounting bolts
- Johnny ring with funnel
- Flathead screwdriver
- Caulking gun and bathroom caulking

1. Empty the tank (see page 16).
2. Lift off the plastic caps and use a wrench to unscrew the bolts at the base of the tank. If the bolts are rusty and corroded, you may have to saw them off using a hacksaw.
3. Lift out the toilet—it's heavy, so bend your knees and lift with your legs (this is when your buddy comes in handy!). You'll have a hole in your floor where the toilet was.

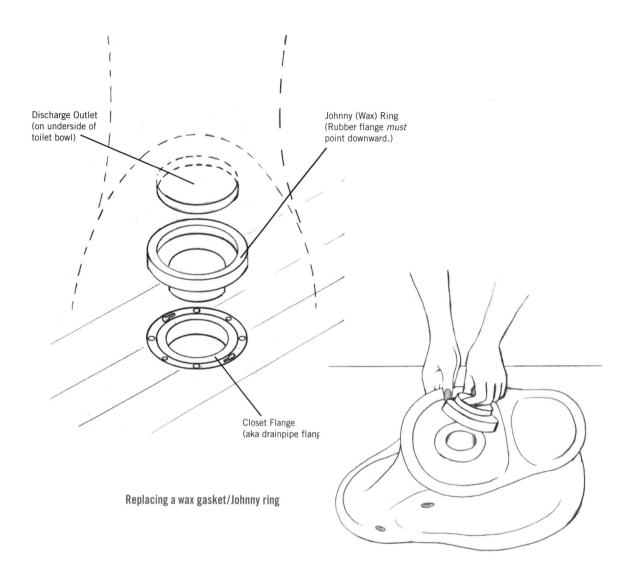

Discharge Outlet
(on underside of
toilet bowl)

Johnny (Wax) Ring
(Rubber flange *must*
point downward.)

Closet Flange
(aka drainpipe flang

Replacing a wax gasket/Johnny ring

4. Tip the toilet over—gently—onto a scrap piece of carpet to expose the bottom of the base.
5. Using a scraper, scrape away the old wax. Pull out the old Johnny ring and wipe the discharge outlet clean. Scrape away the old wax from the floor around the hole where your toilet used to be and wipe the floor clean.
6. Insert new mounting bolts into the closet flange (aka drainpipe flange).

7. Back to the bowl. Place the rounded side of the replacement Johnny ring onto the bottom of the bowl at the discharge outlet, and press it in place so it doesn't fall off when you tip the bowl upright.

8. Lift the bowl and guide it back over the drain so the funnel of the ring goes into the drainpipe and the bolts line up with the holes. This is very tricky, so have patience!

9. Once the bolts are through the holes, press the toilet down, applying pressure all around, to squash the wax, making sure the base of the toilet is flat on the floor.

10. Screw the nuts down, alternately tightening each one a little at a time so the base screws down evenly.

11. Cut the bolts down with a hacksaw so the caps fit, and snap the caps back on.

12. Finally, seal around the base of the toilet with silicone caulking (see "Caulking" 'Round the Tub," page 67).

Chix Chat:

How I Got a Handle on an Embarrassing Situation

You want to talk embarrassing? It's my first visit to my new guy's place. I really like this man, and I am crossing my fingers that his apartment's not hiding any horrors that will change my mind about him. My first impression is positive, so after the initial, "Hello, You look great, nice place," I excuse myself to go to the bathroom.

You can tell a lot about someone by his bathroom. The state of his tub and toilet is a good indicator of his personal hygiene. If his bathroom's clean and fresh, chances are so is he. But if there's moss growing around the edges of his sink . . . proceed at your own risk. If you want to find out what he's really like, do a bit of casual snooping. What's the medicine cabinet stocked with? Beware of too many "anti" products—antifungal creams, anti-itch powders, antidepressants, antibiotics. If there are over ten, run.

So far my guy was batting a thousand. Tidy, nice fixtures, plush towels, moderate amount of men's hair and skin products (never date a guy who has more hair and skin products than you do), and only two "antis"—antiperspirant and antihistamines. Cool. I check my hair, refresh the lipstick, go to the bathroom, flush the toilet—and what happens? The plastic handle breaks off. Just cracks right off. Perfect.

So I'm standing there in his bathroom with the toilet handle in my hand. Now, obviously I have a decision to make. Do I (a) leave it on the floor and pretend nothing happened, (b) try to stick it back on with some extra-firm hair gel, or (c) climb out the window, run home, and change my number?

After careful consideration I chose none of the above. Instead I confidently marched out of the bathroom and said, "Nice bathroom, Jack, but you should have splurged on a more expensive toilet handle." I held it up; he laughed hysterically. What I thought would be a night of embarrassment turned into one wonderful date. And the bonus? That date led to another—a trip to the hardware store, so I could replace his toilet handle . . . with a metal one.

Removing chain

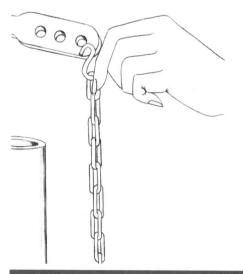

TOILET HANDLES

If your toilet handle is loose, if it's not aesthetically pleasing, or if it breaks clean off, you'll want to replace it. First you must know this: The nut on the inside of the tank connecting to the handle has reverse threads, which means it's threaded in the opposite direction than regular nuts, screws, or fittings. To tighten the nut, you must screw counterclockwise and, to loosen, clockwise.

Toilet handle

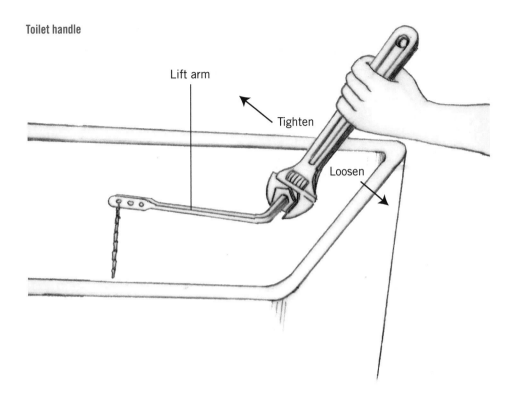

Lift arm

Tighten

Loosen

Replacing or Tightening a Toilet Handle

If the problem with your existing handle is that it's loose, simply tighten the nut with a wrench or pliers, turning *counterclockwise.* But if it's broken or if you just want a new handle, you can follow these simple steps.

TOOLS
- Adjustable wrench or tongue-and-groove pliers

1. Shut off the water supply to the toilet at the shutoff valve and flush twice (see "How to Get Your Tank on Empty," page 16, and follow steps 1 and 2).
2. Disconnect the wire or chain from the lift arm.
3. With the wrench or pliers, unscrew the handle nut (turning clockwise), pull out the handle, and lift the arm.
4. Bring the handle assembly to your plumbing or hardware store—handles come in different lengths and shapes, so you'll need to replace it with the same type.

5. To install the new handle, insert the new lift arm and handle, then screw in the nut (counterclockwise).
6. Reattach the wire or chain to the new lift arm.

Toilet Seats

It's the crowning adornment of your throne, the rest stop for your rump, your derriere's delight—I'm talking about your toilet seat, and the one you've got says a lot about you. Nothing screams "filthy slob" louder than a cruddy toilet seat, so if yours is telling horror stories, it's time to toss it.

When you are installing a new toilet seat, you can choose the color, design, and material (wood, plastic, padded, etc.). What you do not have a choice in is the size and shape of your seat (ain't that the truth!). The seat must fit the shape of your bowl, so before you buy a new seat, determine whether your bowl is round or elongated. You can probably tell just by looking at it, but if you're not sure, take measurements.

Replacing toilet bolts

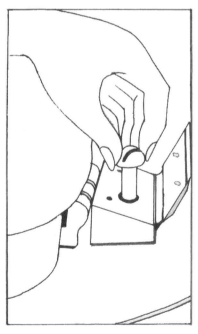
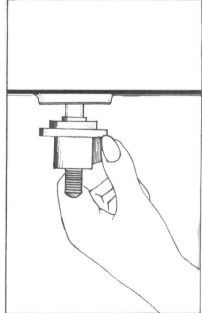

Removing an Old Toilet Seat

TOOLS
- Flathead screwdriver
- Adjustable wrench
- Lubricating spray, as needed
- Hacksaw, as needed

1. Close the lid and unscrew the bolts (they may be hidden under plastic caps, so pry open the cap with a screwdriver).
2. If the screw just spins and doesn't unscrew, you'll need to hold the nut underneath the seat in place with an adjustable wrench so that it doesn't move. If the screws are metal and won't budge, saturate them with lubricating spray, let soak, and come back to unscrew. If they still won't move, you'll have to use a hacksaw to cut the bolt off, which is no easy task!

Installing a New Toilet Seat

TOOLS
- Flathead screwdriver
- Adjustable wrench or tongue-and-groove pliers

1. Clean any buildup that accumulated around the bolt holes.
2. With the lid down, pry up the plastic caps on the hinges (if applicable) with a screwdriver and place the new seat on your bowl so the holes on the set align with those on the bowl.
3. Fit new bolts into the holes and screw the nuts on from the underside of the toilet.
4. When they're snug, hold back each nut by hand or with an adjustable wrench and tighten the bolt with a screwdriver. Do not overtighten the bolts, or you risk of cracking the bolt, the nut, or the porcelain.
5. Raise and lower the lid to make sure the seat is properly tightened—it should move freely but not wiggle around.
6. Snap closed the bolt caps (if applicable) and sit back in comfort!

Unclogging a Toilet

I wish I could tell you there is a magical way to rid your toilet of all the nastiness that's clogging it. A biodegradable, earth-friendly, plumbing-safe tablet that you could simply pop in your bowl to dissolve the clog while transforming the muck into rose water. A neat, easy, *plop-plop, fizz-fizz* that cleans your pipes and has bonus aromatherapy properties besides. If I had a product that would save the world from never having to stick a nasty, splashy plunger or snake in and out of this kind of dis-

Plunging toilet

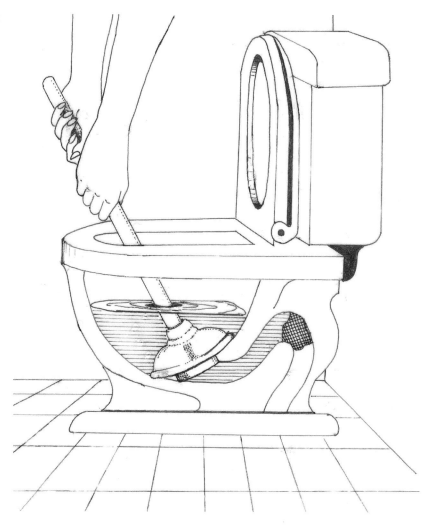

gusting mess again, I would be a very rich woman. But I don't have any magic tablets to offer you. All I can give you is my promise that these tips will make unclogging a toilet as minimally gross and painless as possible.

Toilet clogs are almost always caused by an obstruction in the trap. Using a plunger will create alternating pressure and suction that will loosen the clog and push it through.

Plunging a Toilet

TOOLS
- Air deodorizer (if that doesn't work, you may need incense or even nose plugs)
- Shot of tequila (optional)
- Safety glasses and rubber gloves (if that doesn't work, a hazmat suit)
- Bucket
- Toilet plunger (nozzled shape is specific for toilets, but a regular plunger can work too)

1. First, use whichever air-quality-control method the odor calls for. If necessary, do the tequila shot at this point. Then suit up in safety glasses and gloves.
2. When you plunge, the water in the bowl should be half full (or half empty, if you're a pessimist). If the bowl is empty, add water. If it's full, *do not try to reflush* unless you want that mess all over your floor. Wait for the water to drain slowly. If it doesn't budge, start scooping the contents into a bucket (now's definitely a good time for that shot!).
3. Lift the toilet seat. Insert the funnel of the plunger deep into the bowl and start pumping, up and down about twenty times, with the last stroke being a swift up and out, breaking the suction. This pumping may give you a head rush, especially if you just had some tequila, so repeat as desired, or until the toilet clears.

Chix Tip: Stopping an Overflowing Toilet

If your bowl is about to overflow all over your bathroom floor, quickly turn off the water at the shutoff valve. If there isn't one at the fixture, remove the tank cover and push down on the flapper or stopper, closing the valve seat, which will stop the water.

4. Take your tools outside and spray them down with an antibacterial cleanser and rinse. Let them dry thoroughly before storing them. And what better way to celebrate your fix than with the last of the tequila! Enjoy—you deserve it.

Toilet auger

Getting Through a Serious Clog

If your toilet is still not unclogged and a plunger just isn't working, it's time to try an auger, or plumber's snake. Unlike a plunger, a toilet auger is maneuvered to the clog by way of a long, flexible coil that tears through the obstruction. A toilet auger is designed with a bendable plastic housing around the section of the coil that could scratch your bowl. If this method doesn't work and your clog is too far down the waste line, you'll need to call in a professional.

TOOLS
- Toilet auger (aka closet auger or plumber's snake)
- Bucket

1. Feed the corkscrew tip of the auger down into the drain and begin pressing and turning the handle clockwise, until the entire coil is fed through and the curved, plastic housing is resting at the mouth of the drain.

Word to the Wise

Don't think that because your toilet has a big hole in the bottom of it you can use it like a trash can. Do not flush hair, dental floss, tampon wrappers, paper towels, or any material other than toilet paper.

2. While continuing to turn the handle, slowly pull the coil out. Repeat entire process if necessary. You'll know that the toilet unclogged when the water drains down completely.
3. Once the clog has dislodged, pour an entire bucket of water down the bowl to swill out the debris.
4. Turn the water back on and give it flush. Love that gulp sound! It's clear!
5. Take your tools outside and spray them down with an antibacterial cleanser and rinse. Let them dry thoroughly before storing them.

Augering a toilet

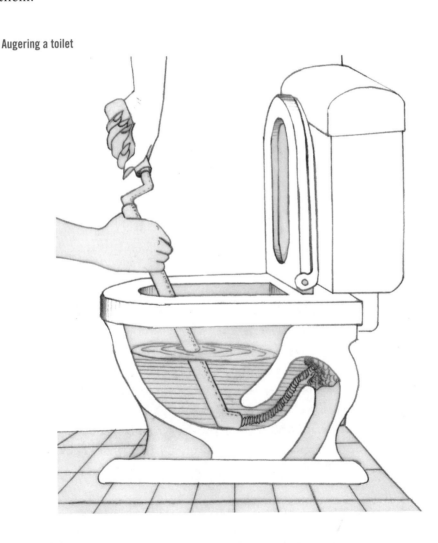

Chix Chat:
My Outstanding Plumbing Bill with Tony Danza

So there I was in New York City, in a dressing room of *The Tony Danza Show*, about to make a live appearance. I'm rifling through my suitcase, which is packed with everything you might imagine a woman like me travels with—wardrobe, beauty products, boots, tool belt, cordless impact driver, pipe wrenches. You know, the usual. (I always imagine what the security inspectors must think when they search my luggage at the airport—"Does this bag belong to a traveling construction worker who dresses in drag, or what?")

I'm nervous—nothing makes me as jittery as live television. There's no, "Cut, let's do that again," like on my show. Live means that what you see is what you get, and my only prayer is that what you get isn't me falling flat on my face.

So I'm searching through my bag to pick out just the right construction boots to go with my outfit. (I brought four pairs with me. You know how we women love our shoes. . . .) I decide on the black pair—leather, steel-toed, really cute. They have to be perfect, so out comes my shoe polish. Do you see where this is going? In an instant, liquid black shoe polish spills all over my hands and pants.

PANIC.

I run to the sink in the dressing room, turn on the water . . . and nothing happens. I turn the knobs on full blast, but only a trickle of water comes out. The freakin' sink isn't working, so I go running for my Channellocks. I've got to fix this faucet!

Wouldn't you know, the producer of the show gets wind of the antics going on in my dressing room and tells Tony. Half an hour later, there I am on live TV with Tony Danza, presenting him with a tool belt (that I loaded with cannolis in case he got hungry), when he says, "So, Norma, I hear you fixed the sink in your dressing room?"

I said, "Yeah, Tony, the bill's in the mail."

Repairing Aerators and Showerheads

"I can't take the pressure!" Lucia was stressed out and venting during our hourlong telephone bitchfest. Job, kids, boyfriend, bills. "My head's about ready to blow off my shoulders!"

We all know the feeling. Pressure wreaks havoc in our body, and if we don't find a healthy way to release it, we can end up with migraines, bad credit, and an addiction to Xanax. I try to avoid pressure at all costs—except in the shower.

Give me pressure! The more the better. Massage my back, stimulate my scalp, invigorate my life! Ever try to rinse out shampoo with a pathetic trickle of water that doesn't have the power to douse a lit match? You leave the shower feeling completely unsatisfied—and not even clean.

That can drive you crazy, but I'll take frustrating over painful any day. You ever take a shower with a showerhead that has only three working holes? The rest are clogged shut, so all that water is being squeezed through those three openings instead of, let's say fifty, with a pressure that simulates a laser cutter—great for tattoo removal, excruciating when you're trying to lather. So whether you have a showerhead that cuts you to ribbons or one that leaves you with a permanent case of hat hair, the pressure is on you to fix it!

And showerheads aren't the only things that get clogged. Sink aerators can be the cause of some pretty erratic water flow. My sink fix in the Tony Danza dressing room was as easy as unscrewing the aerator and tapping out the debris to let water flow through it again. Imagine all the guests who had stayed waterless in that dressing room—a frustration you'll never have to experience once you learn this simple fix.

Unclogging an Aerator

An aerator is the little screwed-on filter screen that attaches to the end of your faucet spout. It's there because if it weren't, the water would chugalug out of the spout and make a big mess. When it becomes clogged, the water will either trickle out or spray in crazy directions.

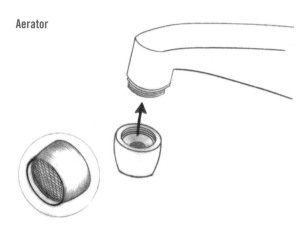

Aerator

TOOLS
- Rubber glove
- Tongue-and-groove pliers
- Teflon tape
- Paper towels
- Old toothbrush, as needed
- White vinegar or demineralizing solution, as needed

1. Grab the tip of your faucet and start turning it clockwise. If it doesn't move, use a rubber glove to help you get a good grip. If it still won't budge, use your pliers. Tape the teeth so you don't mar the faucet finish.
2. Once the aerator is off, run the water. It should flow freely. (If it doesn't, the aerator isn't the problem!) Some aerators have a few parts to them. Remember what order they're in *before* you take them apart, so you know how to put it back together. Tap the aerator upside down onto a paper towel. You'll see all kinds of little mineral granules.
3. If the aerator is really clogged up, scrub it with an old toothbrush. If necessary, soak it in vinegar or demineralizing solution first (read this product's directions and warning label), then brush. (FYI: Depending on the aerator finish, soaking too long may pit the surface.)
4. Screw the clean aerator back on and tighten it by hand. Turn your faucet on. Now, it will flow, flow, flow . . .

Cleaning a Showerhead
Before deciding to replace a showerhead, ask yourself if you used to be happy with it, because if you were, it may be salvageable. A good cleaning will

> ## Chix Trick: One of the Many Marvels of Masking Tape
>
> Keeping small parts from getting lost and staying in order is a great time to get yourself in an annoying situation. Just stick the parts down on a strip of masking tape, placing each piece in the order it's been removed. This trick will make reassembly of the parts super easy.

usually do the trick of ridding a showerhead of all the crusty stuff that has accumulated to mess with your pressure.

TOOLS
- Tongue-and-groove pliers
- Masking tape
- Teflon tape
- White vinegar or demineralizing solution
- Needle

1. Remove the head, using the tongue-and-groove pliers. In order not to scratch the finish on your showerhead, wrap the tips of your tool with masking tape or use a piece of rubber to protect the metal. Place the pliers over the nut of the showerhead. Unscrew the showerhead, turning counterclockwise, while holding back on the shower arm with your hand to prevent it from rotating as you're unscrewing the head.

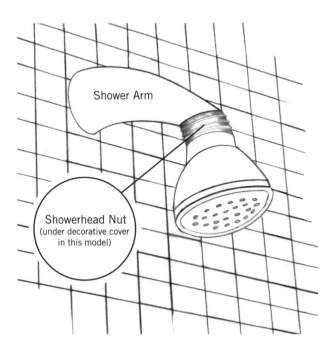

Shower Arm

Showerhead

Showerhead Nut
(under decorative cover
in this model)

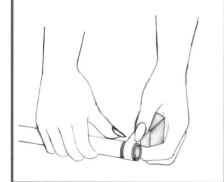
2. Once the showerhead is detached, soak it in white vinegar or a demineralizing solution (read this product's warning label). (FYI: Depending on the showerhead finish, soaking too long may pit the surface.)

3. Rinse water through the showerhead to make sure all the holes are unclogged. You can use a needle to help unclog the holes.

4. Repeat until the water is flowing freely.

5. Remove any old Teflon tape or other gunk that has built up on the shower-arm threads by scrubbing it with a brush.

6. Wrap the threads of the shower arm with Teflon tape clockwise, three or four times.

7. Screw the head on, clockwise, by hand, and then gently tighten it with your wrench.

8. Turn on the water and check for leaks. If there are leaks around the head, tighten some more until properly snug.

Replacing a Showerhead

TOOLS
- Tongue-and-groove pliers
- Masking tape
- Teflon tape
- New showerhead

1. Remove the head, using the tongue-and-groove pliers. In order not to scratch the finish on your showerhead, wrap the tips of your tool with masking tape or use a piece of rubber to protect the metal. Place the tongue-and-groove pliers over the nut of the showerhead. Unscrew the showerhead, turning counterclockwise, while holding back on the shower arm with your hand to prevent it from rotating as you're unscrewing the head.

2. Bring the old showerhead to your plumbing-supply or hardware store to make sure the fit is the same as the one you want to purchase.
3. Attach the new head using the same directions as for replacing a cleaned showerhead.

Replacing a Shower Arm

If that showerhead is just too dirty or if it's time for an upgrade, another option is to remove the showerhead along with its shower arm. This removal means unscrewing the arm from the elbow or stubout (the small pipe coming out of the wall) and replacing the entire unit.

TOOLS
- Tongue-and-groove pliers
- Teflon tape
- Masking tape
- New showerhead and shower arm

1. Holding the base of the shower arm, unscrew the arm from the stubout using both hands or with pliers.
2. Wrap Teflon tape clockwise three or four times around the threads of the new arm. Insert the arm into the stubout—turning clockwise, first thread it in by hand, then tighten with pliers (tape the jaws of your tool with masking tape so you won't mar the arm's finish).
3. Following the steps for replacing a showerhead, screw the new showerhead onto the new shower arm.
4. Turn on the water and check for leaks at both the showerhead connection and the stubout connection. If either one leaks, tighten some more by turning until properly snug.

Chix Tricks: How to Know Which Right Is Right

Do I screw to the left or to the right? The general rule is "righty tighty, lefty loosey." But when you're lying under a sink trying to unscrew something over your face, or leaning over a cabinet trying to screw something from behind, the perspective of clockwise and counterclockwise gets all . . . screwed up.

To solve this problem, here's what you do: Make a thumbs-up sign with your right hand. Hold your thumbs-up next to what you need to screw, pointing your thumb in the direction you want that screw or fitting to move. For example, if you want to remove a screw from a wall, put your thumbs-up next to the screw, with your thumb pointing toward you (so the screw comes *out* of the wall). Now look at the direction your fingers are curling into your palm—that's the direction you need to be turning the screw!

LEAKY FAUCETS

Is there anything more annoying than that incessant dripping from a leaky faucet? *Plip, plip, plip, plip* . . . It makes me want to hurt someone. And there's just no stopping it after a while, right? You've turned the handle so it's as tight as possible, even laid down a washrag in the sink to muffle the sound. Nope, it keeps coming back like razor bumps. There's only one solution—fixing it! But instead of paying a plumber a hundred bucks to change a washer that costs a dollar, you can easily do it yourself!

There are four main types of faucet valves—compression, cartridge, ball, and disk. Each one performs the same function, namely, to control the force of the water and to adjust the mixture of hot and cold. But even though they all do the same thing, the question is, which one do *you* have? Here's the deal: You won't know until you start tinkering with it. So here's a brief course we'll call Valvology 101. Each of these projects will show you how to take your faucet apart, determine which type it is by its parts, and teach you how to repair any leaks.

TOOLS

For all of any of the following faucet fixes, it's best to have all of these tools handy.
- Needle-nose pliers
- Adjustable wrench
- Tongue-and-groove pliers
- Lubricating oil
- Screwdrivers—flathead and Phillips
- Allen wrenches
- Steel wool or scrubber sponge
- Flashlight
- Clean rag
- Valve-seat wrench or seat-dresser tool
  (depending on valve-seat type)

Chix Tricks:
Eight Tips for Faucet Fixin' Chix

Referencing these tips before and during your project will favor a fret-free fix!

1. Before you start unscrewing anything, take a clean washrag and lay it in the sink, covering the drain. If you drop any screws or small hardware, this should catch them before they plunk down out of sight.

2. When turning off the water at the supply valves, observe the leak from the faucet. In a two-handle system, only one side may need repair. You can identify the side by watching which valve stops the leak.

3. When taking parts to the hardware store, put them in plastic bags. They won't get lost, and you won't get dirty.

4. If you are replacing seat washers and are unsure of the correct part, buy one of the frequently available universal kits that contain a dozen or so various seat washers and O-rings. It is likely that one of them will work, and it will save you multiple trips to the hardware store for less than the price of a small decaf 2 percent nonfat latte.

5. If your faucet has any other washers or O-rings not specifically described in the steps listed here, replace 'em while you have it torn apart!

6. If you find that you are forcing something that should be easy, stop and take a look at what you're doing. Even experienced pros can cause costly damage this way. Is there an alignment tab or pin? Are the teeth aligned with the grooves? Is a setscrew not backed out far enough? Try the simple solutions before breaking out the crowbar.

7. If you repair a valve and the faucet no longer drips but water leaks from around the handle, the problem is that the retaining nut either is not tight enough or may be misaligned. Remove the handle again and visually check that the nut is straight. If it is, tighten it a little more with the adjustable wrench.

8. If the previous tip doesn't help much, it may be that the threads around the valve top are worn from age or hard water. You may be able to extend the life of the fixture by wrapping the threads under the retaining nut with a couple of turns of Teflon tape. You will have to shut off the water supply and remove the retaining nut to do this. Make sure that you wrap the Teflon tape in a clockwise direction for standard threads, counterclockwise for reverse threads. This will keep it from bunching up when you put the nut back on.

Fixing a Compression-Valve Faucet

The compression valve is the most common style of faucet, especially in older homes. It is also known as a washer valve or a globe valve. In a compression valve, a central shaft called the valve stem is moved up and down by the turning action of the valve handle. A rubber washer is attached to the bottom of the valve stem with a screw. As the handle turns and the stem and washer move up, a gap is opened that allows

Compression valve

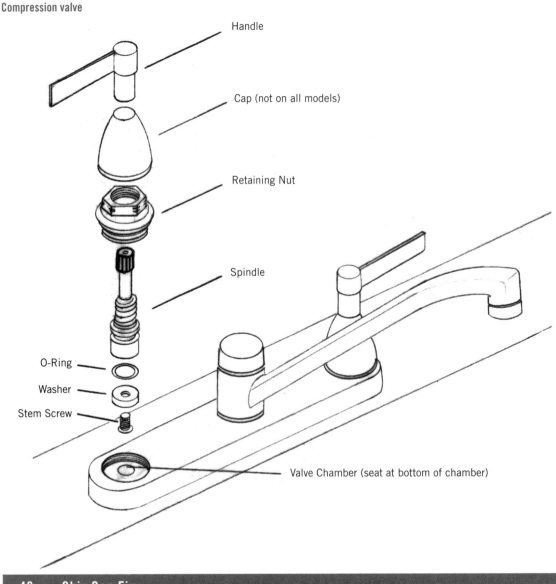

Handle

Cap (not on all models)

Retaining Nut

Spindle

O-Ring

Washer

Stem Screw

Valve Chamber (seat at bottom of chamber)

water to flow. The larger the gap, the stronger the flow. When the valve is fully closed, the washer (called the seat washer) presses, or "sits," tightly against—you guessed it—the valve seat. Once this happens, all's right with the world, and the water stops flowing through your faucet. But this is likely not the case in *your* corner of the world, or you wouldn't be sitting around reading about how to fix your faucet! Here's what you can do to make things right when you have water leaking out of the spout.

1. Turn off the water to your sink, either at the shutoff valves under the sink or at the water main in older homes. Put a rag over the drain so nothing falls in.
2. Remove the sink handles. Typically these are secured in place with a single screw straight down through the center of the knob. The screw may be hidden by a metal or plastic cap. These can be popped off with a small flathead screwdriver or a metal nail file.
3. Once the handles are off, you should be able to identify a retaining nut. It is likely to be fairly large, and you will need a pair of tongue-and-groove pliers or a large adjustable wrench to remove it.
4. Upon removing the retaining nut, you will see the valve-stem assembly. Unscrew the valve in the direction that you would turn the water on. You can use the faucet handle as a lever to remove the valve stem.
5. Look at the washer at the bottom of the valve stem. It will probably be grooved or indented and secured by a single brass screw. If the washer is missing, look for it in the valve chamber and retrieve it with needle-nose pliers. If the washer is missing, split, or corroded, you will have to replace it. To be sure you get the correct replacement washer, take one of the valve stems to the hardware store and ask for help finding the right size.
6. Inspect the valve seat. Run your finger along the seat to check for small imperfections that won't allow it to seal. If you have a defective valve seat you will have to replace it or resurface it, depending on which type of valve seat you have. Some valve seats are remov-

able, which can be replaced, while others are fixed, which can be resurfaced. To determine if you have a replaceable seat, look inside the valve-seat chamber with a flashlight to see if there is a hexagonal or slotted shape in its center. If there is, it's replaceable. To replace it, you'll need a valve-seat wrench.

Insert the wrench into the valve seat and turn counterclockwise to remove the old valve seat. Bring that with you to the plumbing-supply or hardware store for replacement.

If you find that the valve seat has a simple round hole through the center, it is the fixed type and will need to be resurfaced with a seat-dresser tool. Insert the seat dresser firmly into the valve chamber and give it a few turns to "dress" the seat. Visually inspect your progress. When the metal looks like new (it will be bright and shiny), the job is complete. Wipe away any metal shavings with a clean rag before reassembling the faucet.

Seat-dresser tool—
used with a fixed-type seat

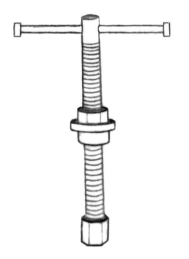

7. Clean the valve stem with steel wool or a plastic scrubber.
8. Install the new seat washer. Make sure the screw is snug, but don't overtighten. This can distort the washer and may cause a leak or premature wear.
9. Reinsert the valve stem into the faucet, turning until it seats completely.
10. Install the retaining nut and tighten with the adjustable wrench.
11. Replace the faucet handles, but don't screw them in yet. Turn the supply valves back on and test the faucet valves. If everything works properly without leaking, install the handle screws and cover plates. That's it!

Fixing a Cartridge-Valve Faucet

Cartridge-type valves may be found in vanity or kitchen faucets. They are more modern than the trusty compression valve. While compact and convenient, cartridge valves are often better off being disposed of rather than replaced, which is unfortunate, due to their expense.

Cartridges are proprietary; each manufacturer has its own design, and designs can vary even among faucets of the same brand. They are often designed to differentiate between hot and cold, and if so are usually color-coded or numbered for reference.

Details aside, when you boil it down, the cartridge valve is little more than a glorified, repackaged version of the compression valve. The procedure to repair a leaky cartridge is similar to that for the compression type. This project details how to fix a double-handle cartridge faucet. Single-handle faucets can have cartridge valves, too, but we'll address them later.

1. Turn off the water at the supply valves. Cover the drain with a rag.
2. Remove the handles. Note that each handle will have an individual cartridge. Use penetrating oil around the base of the handle if it's stuck and pry gently if necessary.
3. Remove the retaining nut (aka bonnet nut).
4. At this point you should be able to pull the entire cartridge out with your fingers. If it is stuck, grab the stem with pliers and try again. The center part may come out separately, or the unit may break. It doesn't matter. The important part is to make sure that you remove all the pieces. Remove the seat and spring with needle-nose pliers.
5. Take the old cartridge to the hardware store to ensure that you buy the right replacement part. Before you go, make a note of the brand of your faucet, as it may not be listed on the part. When shopping for your new part, be sure to read the directions on the package to see if the manufacturer specifies to coat the cartridge with waterproof grease before installing. If so, you will need to buy waterproof grease.
6. To install the new cartridge, apply the waterproof grease if instructed by the manufacturer. Align the tab on the notched part

Cartridge valve

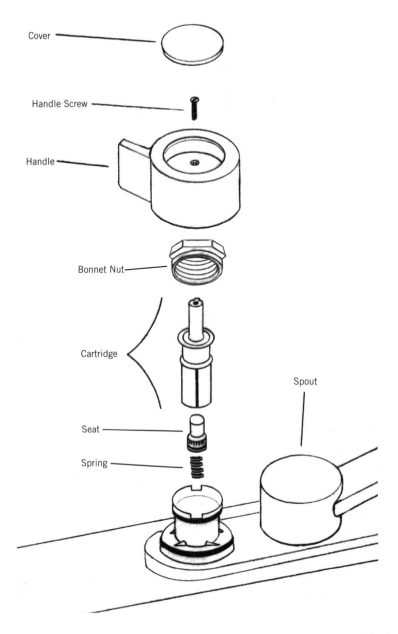

Cover

Handle Screw

Handle

Bonnet Nut

Cartridge

Seat

Spring

Spout

of the faucet housing and press it down firmly. It should slide in without too much force.

7. Replace the retaining nut and snug it with the wrench. Then replace the handle.

8. Turn the supply valve back on and give the faucet a whirl.

Fixing a Ball-Type Valve Faucet

The heart of a ball valve is a cleverly pierced sphere that moves as the handle is tilted and turned. As the holes in the ball align more or less with the water inlets, the flow and temperature are controlled.

Don't be intimidated by this type of fixture. Deep down, it is just like its simpler sisters, and the things that wear it out are no different—moving parts age, rubber gaskets fail; you can begin to see a pattern. To grab this fixture by the ball (heh, heh), follow these simple steps:

1. Turn off the water at the supply valves. Cover the drain with a rag.
2. Inspect the handle and locate the setscrew. You normally don't have to unscrew this completely, just enough to loosen the fit of the handle so that you can remove it. Be careful: because of its small size, this is just the type of screw to get away from you.
3. Unscrew the cap nut, similar to a retaining nut. You may want to wrap this in a towel before unscrewing it to protect the finish, or wrap the jaws of your pliers with masking tape.

Chix Tip:
How to Handle Single-Handle
Compression Faucets, Single-handedly!

Single-handle compression faucets are commonly found in kitchens and baths. In principle, single-handle faucets look and operate just like a cartridge on double-handle models, except that both hot water and cold are channeled through a single valve.

When working on a single-handle fixture, always be sure to turn off both supply valves. To repair a leak, follow the same instructions as for "Fixing a Cartridge-Valve Faucet" on page 49. Keep in mind when dismantling the handles that single handles are usually held in place with a set screw or Allen screw.

Ball valve

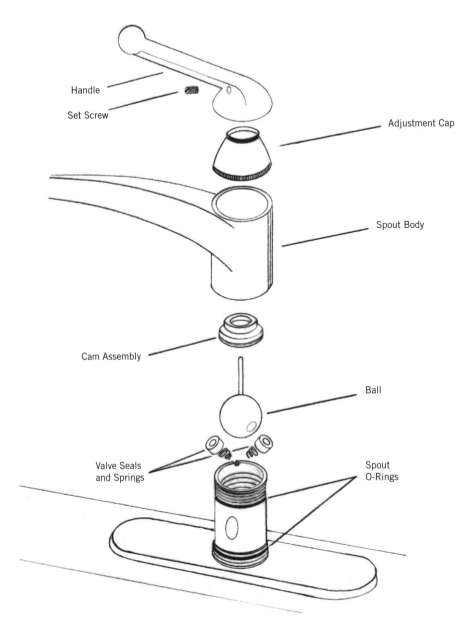

Handle

Set Screw

Adjustment Cap

Spout Body

Cam Assembly

Ball

Valve Seals
and Springs

Spout
O-Rings

4. Remove the cam assembly, the valve seals, and the plastic ball.
Observe the way that these parts come out. They may vary slightly
from the illustrations.

5. Inspect the ball for damage or wear. Sometimes there will be obvious cracks; other times mineral streaking will show age. Frequently the ball will be in good shape and may not need replacement.

6. If you look down into the faucet, you will see two round rubber seals. These are the valve seals, and are the likely culprit of your drip. Using needle-nosed pliers, reach into the faucet and remove these, along with the spring under each one. There will be a seal and spring for hot and a seal and spring for cold.

7. Your plumbing supplier will sell the seals and O-rings for your faucet as a kit (it's always a good idea to bring the old seals with you). You should be able to buy just the seals, but some suppliers force you to buy the ball as well. If you have to buy it, you might as well replace it, whether you need to or not. In fact, if the faucet is leaking from the faucet base, the culprit is probably the O-rings. Systematically go through your faucet and remove and replace all of the rubber parts included in the kit. When replacing an O-ring, don't stretch it like a rubber band to remove it. Instead roll it off the part and install the replacement in the same way. Insert the new seals and springs into the base of the faucet.

8. Replace the ball, the seal washer, and the cam the same way you found them when you took the faucet apart.

9. Replace and tighten the cap nut.

10. Replace the handle and tighten the set screw.

11. Turn the water back on and wash the gook off of your hands.

Fixing a Disk-Valve Faucet

The design of the disk-model faucet is pretty straightforward—a flat disk with holes permits the flow of water as it is moved back and forth. The disk is typically made of a fragile ceramic material, so use care when you handle it.

The nice thing about this style of valve is that simply disassembling and cleaning lime or hard-water deposits from the surface is all you may need to fix it. But if the disk is cracked or chipped, it's a goner and, like the cartridge, must be replaced outright. While you're cleaning, if you discover that your disk or the seals for your faucet are damaged, take the parts to the hardware store to get the correct replacements.

1. Shut off the water.
2. Unscrew the set screw and remove the handle.
3. Lift off the escutcheon cap. This should expose the disk.
4. There are usually three mounting screws holding the disk in place. Remove these and carefully lift the disk out.
5. Turn the disk over and remove the small seals on the bottom. If these look damaged, you will need to replace them.
6. Examine the disk for wear or damage. If the disk is damaged, you will need to buy a new one and replace it.
7. If the disk isn't damaged, clean it thoroughly with a plastic scouring pad and mild detergent. Do not use steel wool or sandpaper, as this may damage the disk. If there are any flaws, you will have to replace it.
8. Replace the seals and place the disk back in the faucet housing.
9. Replace the mounting screws and snug them down.
10. Replace the escutcheon cup.
11. Replace the handle.
12. For this type of faucet, turn the handle on at the faucet in the center position before turning the supply valves back on. This will reduce the chance of damage to the disk by a sudden surge of water.

Disk-valve faucet

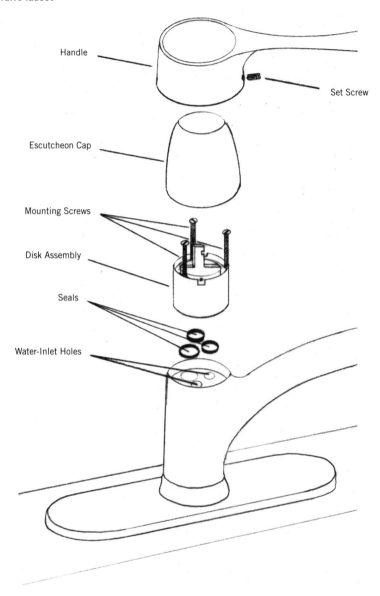

Handle

Set Screw

Escutcheon Cap

Mounting Screws

Disk Assembly

Seals

Water-Inlet Holes

13. If the unit is still leaking, you will have to replace the disk and/or the seals. Bring the used parts to your plumbing-supply or hardware store for replacements and follow steps 8–11.

Fixing Pop-Ups

If your sink's pop-up (the rod that makes the sink stopper go up and down) is too pooped to pop, a few simple adjustments can bring it back to life quickly and easily.

Adjusting your pop-up is a delicate dance of making sure the pivot rod and lift rod are in the right position and properly secured. Interestingly enough, when the stopper rod is pulled *up*, the stopper itself moves *down* (which is the opposite of what you'd think, but then again I'm dyslexic, and that kind of thing confuses the hell out of me). If the retaining nut is too tight, the pivot rod won't move at all. However, if it's too loose, it will leak from that opening when water goes down the drain. As I said, it's a delicate dance. . . .

Cleaning a Pop-Up

When hair's the issue (isn't it always about the hair?), your pop-up won't sit properly in the drain, and instead of forming a seal, it will cause water to leak when you're filling the sink. Sometimes all it takes to fix the problem is a good cleaning.

TOOLS
• Tongue-and-groove pliers

1. Try to pull the stopper out of the drain—this will be easy if it's a floating or loose type. If it won't budge and seems attached to something, reach under the sink and with pliers unscrew the retaining nut, which will loosen the pivot rod. Pull the rod back, releasing the stopper.
2. Clean off all the hair and yucky stuff. If the stopper is beat up, take it to the hardware store to look for the correct replacement.
3. To put the stopper back, reassemble it by following the same steps backward. The only tricky part will be making sure the hole at the bottom of the stopper lines up in the right direction to catch the pivot rod. Be patient and you'll get it.

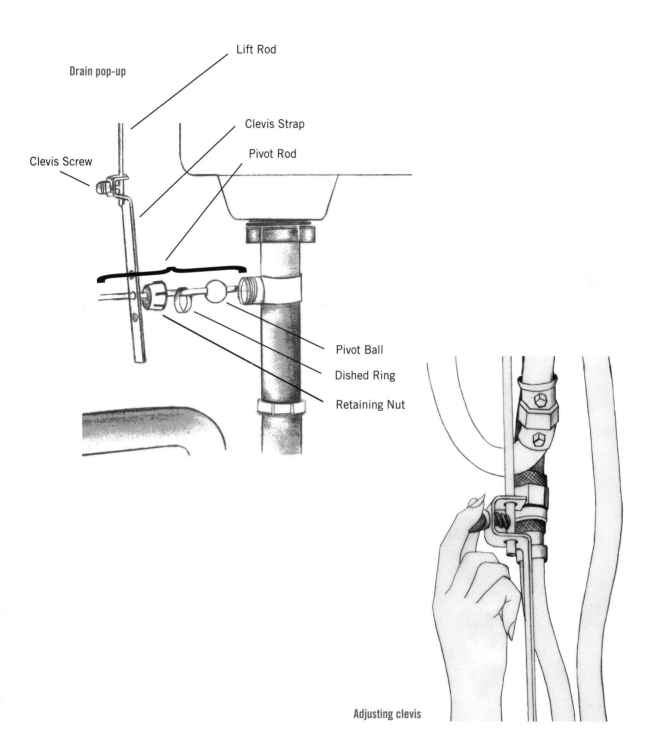

Drain pop-up

Lift Rod

Clevis Strap

Pivot Rod

Clevis Screw

Pivot Ball

Dished Ring

Retaining Nut

Adjusting clevis

Making Adjustments to Your Pop-Up

Like most things over time, moving parts stop moving. They become worn, bent out of shape—you know, the way you feel your first time back to the gym after months of slobbing out on the couch. If your pop-up doesn't work after a cleaning, you may need to adjust the clevis screw, the clevis strap, the spring clip, or the lift rod.

TOOLS
- Your hands
- Tongue-and-groove pliers (if applicable)
- Penetrating oil (if applicable)

1. If the clevis screw has loosened or the clevis strap is bent out of shape, try tightening, bending, or making whatever adjustments necessary while pulling the stopper rod up and down to check if it's working. These adjustments will involve some trial and error.
2. If you can't get it to work, you may need to readjust the position of the pivot rod in the clevis strap. To do so, pinch the small spring clip, pull out the pivot rod, and reposition it in another hole of the clevis strap.
3. Another problem may be that the lift rod needs to be readjusted. Unscrew the clevis screw (if it's stuck, use pliers and penetrating oil). Raise or lower the lift rod, then tighten the clevis screw and check to see if it's in the right position. Repeat this process until the pop-up starts working.

RUB-A-DUB-DUB FOR YOUR SINK AND TUB

Chix Chat:
If It Ain't Broke, You Don't Need to Fix It!

Let me start by saying that the best way to unclog a sink is by preventing the clog in the first place. My aunt Rose-Marie always says it's not the last piece of chocolate you ate that made you fat. Her point being, of course, that it's the *accumulation of behavior over a period of time* (be it hair down the sink, excessive calorie intake, not enough sleep, tolerating negative relationships, or any other bad habit you practice) that will break something or *someone* down—clog them up, drain their energy. You feel me? You know, it's easier to stay healthy than to get well. Let's apply this philosophy to all aspects of our lives—even the freakin' plumbing!

Plunging a Bathroom Sink

The first thing to try on any clog is boiling-hot water poured right down the drain. Sometimes this is all you need! Other times you have to get more aggressive.

TOOLS
- Rag
- Plunger

1. When it comes to unclogging, the best remedy is suction. To create suction, plug the overflow hole of the sink with a rag so air won't escape from it as you plunge.

Plunging sink

2. Take the plunger and put it over the drain. If water isn't completely covering the rubber part of the plunger, add some. Pump up and down about twenty times, with the last stroke being a swift up and out motion that breaks the suction. Repeat until the sink drains.

Removing a P-Trap

The trap under your sink—called a P-trap because of its shape (it looks like a sideways *P*)—is there for two reasons: to prevent noxious sewer gases from seeping into your home (the water creates a barrier) and to catch objects that may fall down the drain (like earrings or other precious items). P-traps are made of metal or plastic, but whatever the material, the function is the same.

TOOLS
- Tongue-and-groove pliers
- Small container or bucket to collect water
- Rubbing alcohol (if applicable)

1. Get under the sink and examine the P-trap. Hand-loosen or use tongue-and-groove pliers to unscrew the nuts at each end of the loop of the trap, but don't unscrew them completely.

P-Trap clean

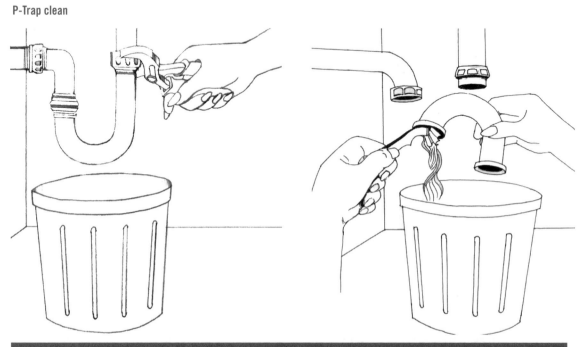

2. Set a bucket, or any container that will fit under the sink, in place under the trap.

3. Unscrew the nuts completely and slide the trap out—any water in the sink will fall into the container.

4. Empty the contents of the P-trap into the bucket—it will be filled with really funky water and gunk. Retrieve anything that may have fallen down the drain, like your earring. Wash out the P-trap (not in *that* sink—no drain, silly). Wash out your earring in alcohol!

5. Screw the P-trap back in place. Keep the bucket under the trap. Pull up the pop-up or cover the drain. Fill the sink with water and then let it all drain out at once. Check for leaks. If the P-trap is leaking, retighten your nuts—maybe you didn't tighten them enough, or maybe they didn't catch the thread properly and went on crooked. Test again and ensure that the trap remains as dry as a whistle.

Chix Safety Tip: Monster in a Bottle— Warnings on Chemical Drain Cleaners

Sometimes chemical drain cleaners can be the perfect quick fix for a clog, but like most quick fixes, they have their drawbacks. If used excessively, chemical drain cleaners can harm your pipes. Here are some things to keep in mind to avoid damage to your drains and yourself:

1. Never use a chemical drain cleaner on a standing clog. The chemical will sit stagnant, causing corrosion to one area of your pipes, and if it doesn't clear the clog, you're left with caustic water that would be dangerous to try to plunge.

2. Never mix chemical drain cleaners. If one is acidic and the other alkaline, the combination can actually cause an explosion or, at the very least, give off toxic fumes.

3. Never look down at the drain after pouring in a chemical cleaner. The chemical reaction with the clog sometimes causes a bubbling up that could hit you in the face!

4. Make sure you are using the right type of chemical for the particular clog you have— some work better with hair as opposed to grease, for example. Read labels.

5. Remember, these chemical drain cleaners are caustic chemicals, so follow all of the manufacturer's safety recommendations.

Unclogging a Kitchen Sink

The procedure for unclogging a kitchen sink is almost identical to a bathroom clog fix, with a few minor exceptions. See pages 59–60 for instructions. Just keep these points in mind:

1. If you have a double sink, you must block the drain of the unclogged side, or the water will shoot up that hole.
2. If you have a food disposal, clamp the line that runs to the air gap or tape a rag around the air gap itself—again, you don't want air escaping, you want suction!

Air gap

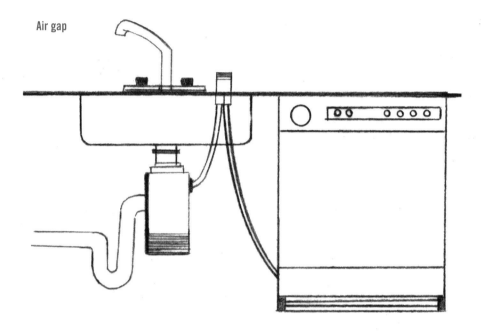

Unclogging a Tub

Soap scum, body soil, dirt, hair—it's a wonder your tub ever drains at all! But if your bathtub is backed up here are a few tips for desludging it. As with any clog, first try pouring boiling water down the drain. If that doesn't work, the most likely culprit causing the clog is hair. So to remove the clog you will need to physically pull out the hair buildup.

Chix Cool Tool: Getting at Tough Clogs with a Plumber's Snake

When plunging, pouring chemical, cursing, and crying don't unclog your drain, it's time to slither and slide that clog right out of your pipes with a plumber's snake (aka trap and drain auger). It's a long metal coil with a crank. Depending on the type of snake, the crank (turning mechanism) might be motorized, driven by a power drill, or manually operated. I suggest buying a good quality manual snake. Motor-driven ones may become overpowering and difficult to control—also, misuse could damage your pipes.

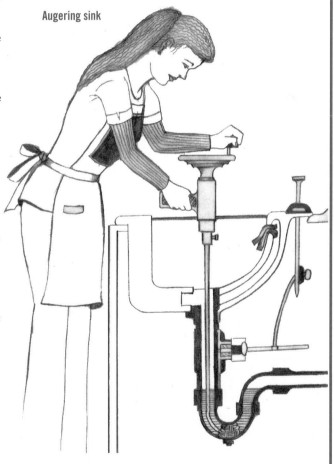

Augering sink

To use, insert the tip of the snake down the drain of your sink and feed the coil, rotating the handle clockwise, pushing in slightly. If the sink is drained, adding hot water will help loosen the clog as you're snaking, so half fill the sink with water. Keep going until you hit resistance. Continue feeding the snake through the clog and swiftly pull back and rotate out. If the handle becomes too hard to turn, pull out the snake by winding the coil back, turning the handle counterclockwise. Clean off any debris that may be stuck on the end and reinsert down the drain. Continue this process until the snake moves freely and running water passes.

A manual plumber's snake can also be used to unclog toilets and shower and bath drains.

Chix Tricks: Get Rid of Plastic Hair Catchers

Plastic hair catchers to place over a shower strainer sound like a good idea, but in my experience they move around and don't allow the water to drain properly as you're showering. My advice is to try to collect your hair in your hand while you're rinsing. Roll it up in a ball and throw it out in the garbage after you shower. Just don't throw it in the toilet — you should know better than that!

Cleaning Out a Tub Drain

TOOLS
- Waterproof gloves
- Rag
- Phillips and flathead screwdrivers
- Needle-nose pliers
- Wire hanger
- Plastic bag

1. Put on waterproof gloves to protect your hands. Cover the drain with a rag to make sure nothing falls into it and put down a towel in the tub so you don't scratch it with your tools.
2. If your tub has a strainer, unscrew the strainer grate (if screws are present). If there are no screws, use needle-nose pliers to remove the entire strainer grate.
3. With pliers, bend the tip of a wire hanger into the shape of a hook. Fish the hanger down the drain and pull up the wad of hair causing the clog. Discard the debris in a plastic bag. This will take a few tries. I'm warning you, what you pull out will look and smell like a slimy alien baby.
4. Flush with hot water. If the water doesn't flow freely, keep fishing until it does.
5. Replace the strainer.

Cleaning a Tub's Pop-Up Stopper

TOOLS
- Waterproof gloves
- Rag

1. Lift the trip lever.
2. Pull out the stopper assembly (making note of the direction of the rocker arm). Pull off the hair and debris and wipe clean with a rag.

3. Reinsert the assembly with the rocker arm in the same orientation as it was (the outward curve of the rocker arm should be facing the inside of the tub).
4. Flush with hot water, and the water should flow freely. If not, try plunging. . . .

Plunging a Tub

TOOLS
- Rag
- Plunger

1. Plug up the overflow hole in the tub with a rag.
2. Take the plunger and put it over the drain. If water isn't covering the rubber part of the plunger, add some.
3. Pump the plunger up and down about twenty times, with the last stroke being a swift up and out, breaking suction. Repeat until tub drains.

Replacing a Tub Spout

The shower in the guest bathroom of my mom's house was a disaster. You've seen showers like these, where you have to pull up a knob on the tub spout (called a diverter) to redirect the water flow to the shower-head. Well, when I pulled up the diverter in my mom's bathroom, more water would leak from the tub spout than would flow from the showerhead! Water would gush over my ankles, but I'd barely have a trickle coming down from above. I'd finish my shower with the cleanest feet in the business—and my hair still full of shampoo.

Lucky for us, changing a tub spout, whether it's leaky like my mom's or just

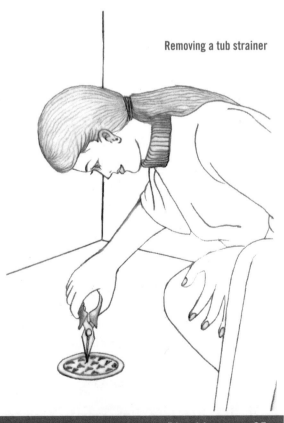

Removing a tub strainer

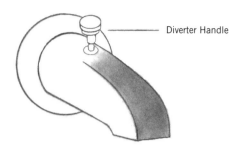

Diverter spout

Diverter Handle

old and grimy, is a super-easy project. You'll first need to identify if your spout is a threaded or slip type. A threaded spout is exactly that, threaded, and screws onto the pipe that comes from the wall, which is called a nipple (yeah, I know). A slip spout fits over the nipple and fastens with a set screw. No matter which type of spout it is, if it has a diverter on it, you'll have to replace it with a diverter spout as well.

Replacing a Slip Spout

TOOLS
- Allen wrench or screwdriver, flathead and/or Phillips
- Replacement spout
- Rag
- Caulking gun and bathroom caulking

1. Look under the spout toward the wall for a slot where the screw is accessible. You'll need either an Allen wrench or a screwdriver to loosen the screw. Once it's loosened, just slip it off—hence the name!
2. Take the spout with you to the hardware store for the right replacement. Compare lengths. It's not the exterior length that counts but rather the length inside the spout, where the gasket of a slip joint starts.
3. Back in your bathroom, clean any old caulking or plumber's putty residue off the nipple with a rag.
4. Slide the new spout over the nipple and tighten the setscrew.
5. Apply a small bead of bathroom caulking around the back end of the spout, creating a neat seal at the wall (see "Caulking 'Round the Tub," page 67).

Replacing a Threaded Spout

TOOLS
- Replacement spout
- Teflon tape
- Caulking gun and and bathroom caulking

1. Unscrew the entire spout by hand, counterclockwise.
2. Take the spout with you to the hardware store for the right replacement. Compare lengths. It's not the exterior length that counts, but rather the length inside the spout, where the threads start.
3. Wrap plumber's tape clockwise around the threads of the nipple.
4. Screw on the new spout.
5. Apply a small bead of bathroom caulking around the back end of the spout, creating a neat seal at the wall (see "Caulking 'Round the Tub," below).

Caulking 'Round the Tub

Taking a bath is one of the simplest yet most luxurious treats you can give yourself. I light candles, play music, and pour a glass of wine. But that's all outside the tub—you should see what I put inside! Bubble bath, oils, bath salts, herbs—it looks like I'm simmering in a vat of soup. I love my baths, but there is one thing I don't like.

Ever take a bath and get the feeling you're being watched? You look around and there they are, in your caulking. The Mold 'n' Mildew Brothers—and they're looking to jump into the tub with you! And no matter how much you try scrubbing and bleaching, they just won't go away. That's when it's time to pull out your caulking gun and blast those bad boys right out of your bathroom.

The Caulk Fix

Make sure you buy caulking that resists mildew and is waterproof. It's available in both water and silicone bases. Silicone caulking may be more resistant than water-based, but it's more difficult to work with because it doesn't wipe up with water.

TOOLS
- Razor scraper
- Disinfectant bathroom cleanser
- Caulking gun and caulking
- Wire hanger
- Paper towels, or rag
- Baby oil

Caulking gun

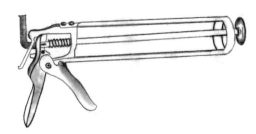

Chix Tricks:
Caulking

This caulking technique applies to all types of caulking jobs, like around a sink, the base of a toilet, a tub spout, a window, or even around molding, using painter's caulking! Just adapt the steps to fit your particular project.

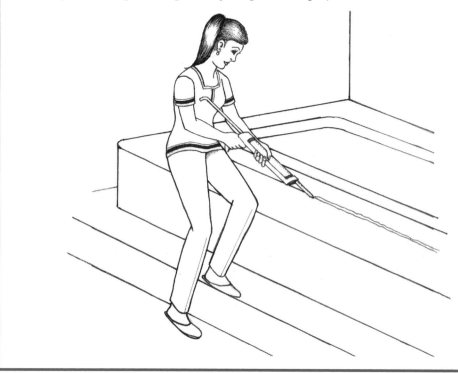

1. Scrape out the old caulking, being sure to hold the razor scraper at an angle so you don't scratch the tile.
2. Wipe down the area and clean with disinfectant cleanser.
3. If the joint seems damp (it may smell musty), you must let it dry before applying the caulking.
4. Load the gun, pierce the seal in the caulking tube with the wire hanger, push the plunger forward, and squeeze the trigger to get caulk to the tip of the gun.

5. Run a thin bead of caulking along the joint and then smooth it down by gliding your finger along the length of the joint. Wipe the excess off your finger on a paper towel or rag as you work. Keep your finger moist with water (if using water-based caulking) or baby oil (if using silicone) to help smooth out the caulking. While wiping, release the plunger so the caulking doesn't continue to ooze out.

6. Continue this process of caulking and wiping on each side of the tub.

7. Let the caulking dry according to the manufacturer's suggested drying time before you use the tub again. In other words, don't touch it or get it wet until it's fully dry.

> ## Chix Tricks: Get Out Your Hair Dryer
>
> You can use a blow dryer to speed up drying time of your tub joint before and after caulking.

HOT-WATER TANK MAINTENANCE

The life of a hot-water tank, aka water heater, can be extended and run more efficiently if you follow a few simple tips.

Flush your tank annually to clear out the sediment that accumulates on the bottom of the tank. Over time this accumulation will reduce the tank's heating efficiency and risk contaminating the water. The sediment is the result of mineral deposits and other particles from our water. When that debris heats up, it may create undesirable chemical compounds—hence the advice that one shouldn't drink hot water from the faucet.

Flushing the Tank

Be aware that a thin plastic hose or bucket used for draining the hot water will become very soft and malleable. Be careful not to burn yourself! If the drain valve becomes clogged with debris while draining, open the cold-water valve to help push the debris through.

Hot-water tank with drain valve

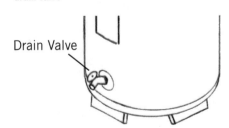

Drain Valve

TOOLS

• Garden hose
• Bucket

1. If the tank is electric, shut off the power to it from your electric service panel. If it's gas, turn the control knob to the "off" position.
2. Turn off the cold water running to the tank.
3. Attach a garden hose to the drain valve found at the bottom of the tank and position it to drain down a utility sink, into a sump-pump hole or sturdy bucket, or out of the garage.
4. Open the hot-water faucet of any sink, then open the drain valve on the tank—it will start draining!
5. When water stops draining, shut off the drain valve and open the cold valve to the tank to flush out stubborn sediment.
6. Shut off the water, open the drain valve again, and continue draining. Repeat if necessary.
7. Once the water runs clear, close the drain valve, open the cold-water valve, and fill the tank until the water from the hot-water faucet begins running.
8. Turn your electricity back on at the service panel or turn on the gas (see "Relighting the Pilot Light," below). Celebrate, you have a clean tank!

Pilot lighting

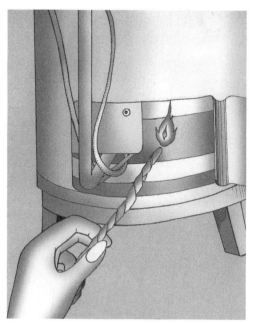

Relighting a Pilot Light

If you smell gas near your water heater or aren't getting any hot water, check to see that your pilot light is still lit. In addition to the following steps, refer to the pilot-lighting instructions in your owner's manual or on the water heater's label. Be advised: If the smell of gas is overwhelming, shut your gas from the main gas shutoff (see Chix Tip: Got Gas?, page 74) and call a serviceperson.

TOOLS
- Flathead screwdriver or pliers
- Match or long-nose lighter

1. Turn the control knob to the "off" position. Wait a few minutes for any residual gas to clear.
2. Remove the panel(s) that encloses the pilot, using a flathead screwdriver or pliers.
3. With a match or long-nose lighter in hand, turn the knob to the "pilot" position, press it down, and put the flame to the tip of the pilot. (Check the owner's manual for your hot-water heater to locate the correct knob or reset button.) The pilot should light.
4. Hold the pilot button down for about a minute, then slowly release. It should stay lit.
5. If it goes out, repeat steps 3 and 4, only hold down the button for a longer period of time. If it blows out again, try once more. If the problem persists, turn the knob to the "off" position and call a serviceperson.

How Hot Is Hot?

The U.S. Department of Energy recommends a home hot-water temperature of 120 degrees. Testing the temperature of your water is easy—just stick a cooking thermometer into a deep cup filled with your faucet's hottest water.

But what the Department of Energy doesn't realize is that I love a really hot shower. I'm talkin' eye-popping, sweltering come-out-looking-like-a-steamed-lobster *hot*. So go ahead and dip me in butter and serve me with a side of corn on the cob—I'm not lowering my temperature. There are some drawbacks to keeping your water too hot, however. The worst is you run the risk of being scalded. Additionally, your fuel bills may be higher than you're happy with.

Keeping your temperature much lower than 120 degrees, however, can backfire on you, too. Think about it: With a lower temperature, you'll mix less cold water to achieve a comfortable temperature, which means you run out of hot water sooner. That won't work in a household that needs lots of hot water available so everyone can leave the shower happy.

Adjusting Temperature on an Electric Hot-Water Tank

TOOLS
- Phillips or flathead screwdriver

1. Turn off the power to the tank from your electric service panel.
2. Refer to the owner's manual and locate the thermostat(s).
3. Electric tanks may have one or two thermostats and will be behind a panel. Remove the panel and any insulation.
4. With a screwdriver, turn the thermostat-control dial to your desired temperature.
5. If there's a reset button, hit it, put back the insulation, and reattach the panel.
6. Turn the power back on at the service panel.

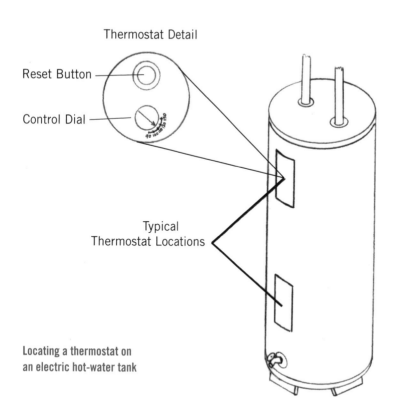

Thermostat Detail

Reset Button

Control Dial

Typical
Thermostat Locations

Locating a thermostat on
an electric hot-water tank

Adjusting Temperature on a Gas Hot-Water Tank

TOOLS
- Flathead screwdriver or pliers

1. Refer to the owner's manual and locate the thermostat at the bottom of the tank. Some tanks hide the thermostat behind a small panel—remove the panel to expose it (you may need a screwdriver or pliers to pry it off).
2. There will be a marked control knob that indicates temperature settings using color, words, or numbers.
3. Turn it to your desired setting.

Adjusting Temperature on an Oil Hot-Water Tank

1. Locate the control knob at the side of the tank and adjust it to the desired setting.

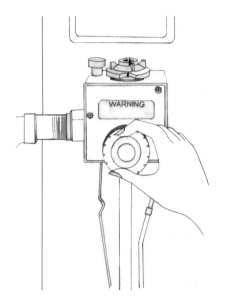

Gas water heater thermostat

MAKING REPLACEMENTS: FLEXIBLE SUPPLY LINES AND SHUTOFF VALVES

Water-supply lines run from every fixture and appliance in your kitchen and bathroom to a supply pipe that comes from behind the wall or floor. The supply lines may be rigid or flexible. Flexible supply lines, aka tubing, are easy to replace.

Replacing Flexible Water-Supply Lines

When one of these supply lines leaks from the fitting or becomes dried out and rotted (like the lines on Aunt Rose-Marie's washing machine that ruptured and spouted like Mount Vesuvius all over the kitchen) they must be replaced—the sooner the better! My favorite flexible supply lines to work with are made of braided stainless steel, also called "no-burst" (you see why they're my favorite?). They're a brushed-nickel color that also happens to look great.

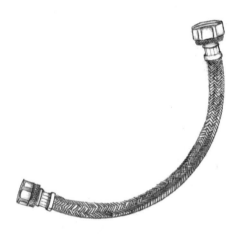

Braided line

Chix Tip: Got Gas?
Labeling Your Gas Utility

I'm convinced that gremlins exist. Nasty little devils who sneak through your house when you're not there, filling their pockets with all the things you don't notice are missing until you need them and they're gone. Misplaced keys and sunglasses. *One* disappearing earring (you know they were both there when you took them off!). Missing scrunchies and hair clips (I swear I've bought thousands over the years and can never find one when I need it). All these things I blame on the gremlins.

I say we should stand up and unite against them. If any one of us ever catches one of these little bastards in the act, let's make an example of him and hold a public execution.

Main gas shutoff valve

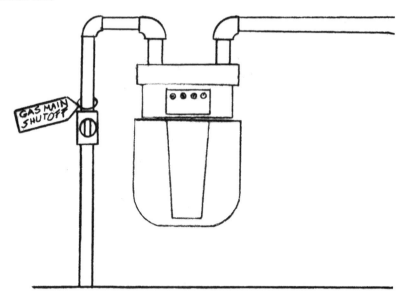

How about when you get a load of laundry out of the dryer and one of your socks is missing? Who could have taken it but the gremlins? I'm always pulling the dryer away from the wall looking for the missing sock that's never there. The trouble comes when you yank on the dryer just a wee bit too hard and pull the gas line loose. Next thing you know, your house smells like gas. What do you do?

The gas meter has a main shutoff valve that cuts off the gas to the entire house. Label it! If you ever smell gas and can't figure out where it's coming from, call your gas company, open the windows, turn off any appliances or lights, make sure not to light a match, grab your wrench, and go shut off your gas main.

How do you know when a valve is in the "off" position? Here's a little rule to follow: If the handle crosses the line/pipe, it's off, cutting the flow. If it's parallel with the line/pipe, it's on, or in line with the flow. If the valve is a gate valve with a round handle, remember this rule: Lefty loosey, righty tighty (turning to the left loosens or opens the valve, turning to the right closes it).

Know where your gas shutoffs are and you won't ever have to worry about leaks. Now all you have to worry about are those missing socks!

Gas shutoff valve in on/open position

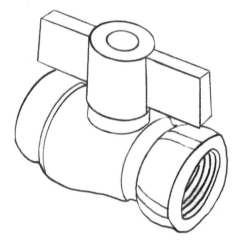

Flexible supply lines are available in different lengths, so you need to know the distance from the shutoff valve to the fixture before you buy a replacement line (if you're not sure, get one that's longer—you can always loop the excess). Also, specify to the salesperson what the line is for, since your washing machine, toilet, sink, et cetera, all have different-size fittings. Your best bet is to take the old tubing with you.

TOOLS
• Tongue-and-groove pliers

1. Turn off the shutoff valve that supplies the particular fixture or appliance you're working on. If it's at a sink, open the faucet to empty out the line and then shut the faucet.
2. With tongue-and-groove pliers, unscrew the fitting at the shutoff, then the fitting at the fixture or appliance.
3. Screw on the new line, first by hand, then giving it one turn with your pliers. Sometimes a toilet supply line has a plastic wingnut that should be tightened only by hand. Do not overtighten—if you do, you'll squash the washer inside the fitting, causing it to lose its ability to create a seal.
4. Turn on the shutoff valve and check for leaks. If the line is dripping from one of the fittings, give the supply-line fitting another twist with the pliers to snug a bit more—that will do the trick.

Replacing a Shutoff Valve

Okay, you're all excited to start your plumbing project. *Step 1. Turn off the water from the shutoff valve.* Easy enough. Wait a minute—the shutoff valve is leaking like a sieve! Now what am I supposed to do?

Here's the deal: You need to replace it. If you have one of the common shutoff valves (as described below) and are prepared to have **all the water in your house shut down for several hours** . . . you can do this project! Yes, it's challenging, but isn't anything worthwhile a challenge? Just be advised that if something goes wrong and you can't get the new shutoff valve on, you will have to keep the water main off until after calling in a professional. If the worst happens, look at it this way:

You'll at least have had a professional plumbing lesson on why you couldn't get it to work right.

TOOLS
- Adjustable wrench
- Tongue-and-groove pliers
- Flashlight
- Hacksaw, PVC cutter, or pipe cutter
- Sandpaper or steel wool and rags
- Teflon tape (if applicable)
- Plumber's phone number—just in case!

1. To get started, take a good look at the fitting below the shutoff valve (you may need a flashlight). It will be either a soldered connection, a screwed-on fitting, or a compression fitting. To determine the proper replacement, you will need to remove the old valve and bring it with you to your hardware or plumbing store.

2. Turn off the water supply to the house (see "Locating Your Water Main," page 13).

3. With tongue-and-groove pliers, unscrew and disconnect your supply lines.

4. **If your valve screws on:** Unscrew it with an adjustable wrench. Screw on the replacement valve and skip to step 11.

   If your valve is soldered on: It will look like it's slipped on the pipe. Cut the pipe just below the existing valve. You can use a hacksaw, a PVC cutter, or a pipe cutter, as appropriate. The right cutter will sometimes depend on how much space there is where you're cutting (see "Using a Hacksaw," page 23). Try to make the cut straight across the pipe. Don't cut it too close to the wall, or you won't be able to

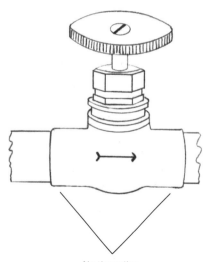

Soldered valve

No threading
(appears to be slipped on,
with silver residue in joints)

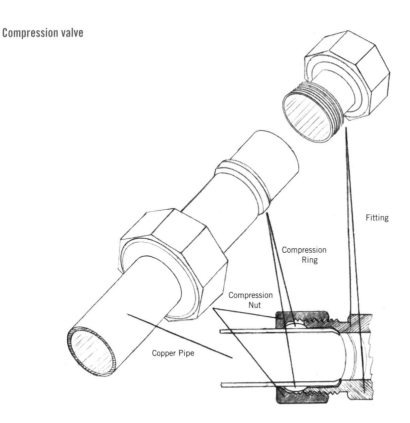

Fitting

Compression
Ring

Compression
Nut

Copper Pipe

install the new valve—leave enough pipe to attach the new valve. With a new tip on the end of the pipe, you'll be ready to install a compression fitting—no soldering necessary.

If your valve is a compression fitting: It will look like it can be unscrewed. With an adjustable wrench, twist the nut, while with another wrench hold back on the pipe stub it's attached to (so you don't yank and damage any connection behind the wall or distort the roundness of the pipe). Twist and pull off the old fitting. There may be a compression ring left on the pipe. Slide it off. If the ring is metal (as opposed to plastic) and really stuck on there, just leave it there for your new valve to fit over. If there is enough pipe exposed to fit the new valve, you could also simply cut off the valve with a pipe cutter or hacksaw and start from scratch. (See "Using a Hacksaw," page 23.)

5. Take the pieces to the hardware or plumbing store to ensure that you buy a valve that fits the pipe diameter for your project.

6. To install your new compression fitting, first use sandpaper or steel wool to clean the end of the pipe where the valve will fit.

7. Slide the compression nut over the water line.

8. Slide the compression ring over the water line (unless using the old ring—see "If your valve is a compression fitting" in step 4, above).

9. Slide the new valve over the water line. Position the handle for easy access.

10. Tighten the compression nut against the valve. Use an adjustable wrench to snug this connection. If your plumbing supplier recommends it, use a little Teflon tape on the threads.

11. Reconnect the supply line(s) connecting the valve(s) to the faucet(s) (see "Replacing Flexible Water-Supply Lines," page 73).

12. Turn the water back on and check the new valves for leaks. If you see any seepage, tighten the connection a little more. If this doesn't solve the problem, turn the water back off and examine the fitting for damage.

Electricity

Electrical projects used to scare me to death, and I can actually pinpoint the exact moment I started being afraid of electricity. When I was ten years old, I learned in school that water conducts electricity. I somehow got the bright idea of proving this to my brother, Roberto. I figured that if I created a gap in an electrical circuit and filled it with water, I could show him how the electricity would continue to flow.

So, genius that I was, I took a lamp, cut the cord, placed the lamp end of the cord into a glass of water, and plugged the other end into an outlet. I thought if I then placed the live end into the same glass of water, the lamp would light. Sounds great, right? Wrong. I put the live end of the cord into the water and—BOOM! The glass exploded!

When I grabbed the cord to yank it out of the outlet, there was a second boom . . . and what happened after that, I couldn't really tell you. All I know is that the outlet never worked again . . . and my hair went from straight to curly and hasn't uncurled since—except when it's blow-dried straight.

With that childhood trauma floating around in the back of my curly little head, you can understand why opening up an outlet would make me nervous It's good to have a healthy fear of something that can hurt you. What's not good is if you let that fear paralyze you and keep you from accomplishing a project. How I got over my fear was through knowledge. Here's the thing: As long as you take the necessary precautions—namely, making sure the power is off—working on an electrical project is 100 percent safe. So let's conquer that fear of the unknown and get into some electric basix.

ELECTRIC BASIX: UNDERSTANDING HOW
ELECTRICITY FLOWS IN YOUR HOME

Electricity travels from the utility company, enters your home, runs through the electrical meter, and then branches off in the service panel. Most homes today have a three-wire service, which means that the utility company provides two "hot" wires and one neutral. A hot wire carries approximately 110 to 120 volts, while the neutral wire returns the path of electricity through the system, creating a circuit. (The spread between 110 and 120 exists because voltage fluctuates as it travels from the utility company into your home. For consistency, from now on I'll refer to the hot wires as 110 lines.) Almost all appliances run on 110 volts, but larger appliances, like a dryer or an air-conditioning unit, may require two 110-volt wires, hence a 220 line (110 + 110 = 220).

In your service panel, whether it's a circuit breaker or fuse type, each of the 110 lines runs to a hot "bus bar," and the neutral line goes to a neutral bus bar. Hooked into the hot bus bars are the breakers or fuses that feed electricity and distribute hot wires to all of your outlets, switches, and appliances. Connecting into the neutral bus bar are all of your neutral wires, which return electricity from each receptacle in order to create a closed circuit. The neutral bus bar grounds all of the neutral wires through a continuous grounding electrode that brings them in direct contact with the earth (ground), often via the pipe of the water main.

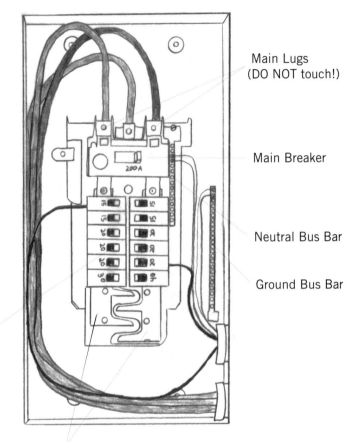

Service panel

Interior
(minimal circuitry shown for clarity)

Main Lugs
(DO NOT touch!)

Main Breaker

200 A

Neutral Bus Bar

Ground Bus Bar

Circuit Breakers

Hot Bus Bars with Space
for Additional Breakers
(DO NOT touch!)

Mapping Your Electric Utility

Mapping your service panel—labeling every circuit breaker or fuse
with its corresponding outlet, switch, light fixture, or appliance—is an
absolute must. Mapping is tedious and time-consuming, but once it's
done, it's *done,* and you never have to worry about it again.

There should be a layout on the inside door of your electrical service panel box that is already numbered to correspond with each breaker or fuse. Unfortunately, the space given to write what each breaker controls is tiny—the labeling works if that breaker is dedicated to just one appliance, like "refrigerator," but when you have to write "hallway, bathroom outlets, and outlet on south side of guest bedroom," you're screwed. That's why I like to draw up my own plan.

Before getting started, shut off any equipment that may be damaged by a power-out, like a computer. Then begin by numbering each breaker or fuse with a blank label—applying the label either onto a piece of tape directly on the breaker or onto the plan provided on the panel door. Now you can trace the general circuits in your home through the process of elimination. Turn on an overhead fixture or lamp in every room, trip a breaker or disconnect a fuse, and note which light shuts off. This will locate the circuit for that room. Now that you've identified the room and one of its breakers, continue testing each outlet in that room with either a lamp or radio to see if each outlet is connected to the same breaker. (A radio is a great outlet tester, because even if you're alone, you can hear it go off when you trip the right breaker.) If one of the outlets works in the room where your identified breaker is off, you must switch off every breaker until you locate the one that connects to that particular outlet. On a separate sheet of paper, write down the breaker or fuse number that corresponds with each fixture or outlet. Depending on the size of your home, going back and forth from the service panel to each room can become an aerobics session, so you might as well go ahead, put your sneakers on, and make it a real workout.

Safety Musts: I'm Not Asking— I'm *Telling* You to Read This!

Now that you have an understanding of how electricity flows, let's be clear on how never to let it flow to you! Electrical projects can be dangerous, even lethal, unless you *strictly* follow these safety precautions:

1. Before starting any electrical project, turn off the electricity from the service panel. (This should be easy if you mapped your service as discussed above).

2. Even with the breaker/fuse off, handle the wires and terminals as if they were hot until you run a second check with an electricity tester. The easiest and most versatile to use is a pen-type voltage indicator. Simply touch the wires and terminals with the probe of the tester or, for an outlet, point the probe in the smaller or right-hand slot of the receptacle (the "hot" side)—the tester light will shine if there is current. These devices run by battery, so check that yours is working by testing it on an outlet you know has power.

Turning off main breaker

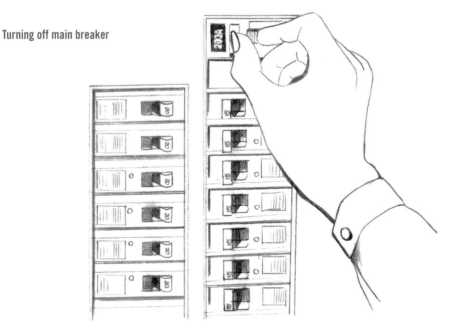

3. Do not touch your service panel with both hands—you could receive a shock, since your body would be creating a closed circuit if both hands touch the panel at the same time. So always keep one hand at your side.

4. Put a piece of tape over the breaker/fuse to be sure no one accidentally turns it back on while you're working.

5. Always recap wires with wire nuts while working, even though you know the power is off.

6. Be sure an appliance or fixture is unplugged before you start to repair it.

7. Water and electricity don't mix! Be aware of your surroundings and be sure you're not standing in any water.

Touching service panel

WIRE: CUTTING, STRIPPING, AND JOINING

When handling an electrical project, you will come across different thicknesses of wire, called AWG (American Wire Gauge). The thicker the wire, the lower the gauge and the more current it can carry. Most homes are wired with AWG 12 or 14. The core of typical household wire is made of copper, either solid or stranded (made of many thin wires that together create the core) while the exterior sheathing is made of a protective plastic. You'll see these types of wires in almost any electrical project, whether it's changing an outlet or hanging a light fixture.

So before starting an electrical project, you need to become familiar with cutting, stripping, and joining wire.

Cutting Wire

Cutting wire is easy. It's like cutting rope, but instead of scissors you use lineman's pliers or wire cutters. What's important when cutting wire is to be sure that you cut far enough along the wire to remove the old, damaged end, leaving a fresh wire end—similar to cutting off split ends when you trim your hair. When wiring a project, you always want to use a wire end that isn't frayed.

Wire cutter

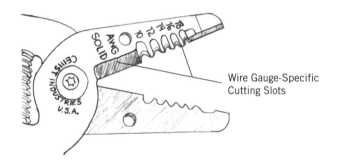

Wire Gauge-Specific Cutting Slots

TOOLS
• Wire cutters or lineman's pliers

Stripping Wire

Stripping wire—cutting away the plastic while leaving the core intact—can be tricky if you don't have the right tool, namely, a wire stripper. If you don't have a wire stripper, you can strip wire with a wire cutter or utility knife. This involves gently cutting the plastic while turning the wire until you break through the plastic sheathing. Then you can simply pull the sheathing away from the core. Stripping wire is a must when you need to expose the metal core in order to join the wire to another wire or to an outlet or a switch.

TOOLS
- Wire stripper

1. With a wire stripper, insert the wire in the corresponding size cutting slot.
2. Snip and pull away plastic sheathing.
3. Voilà! The metal core is intact and ready to be used for your project.

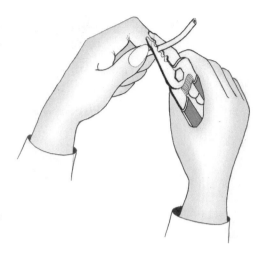

Stripping wire

Joining Wire

When joining wire you'll use a wire nut (aka wire cap) to cap the connection. Wire nuts come in different colors and sizes. The thicker the wires, the larger the nut you'll need to join them. The nut is threaded inside to bite into the wires you're connecting as you screw them together. Once the nut joins the wires, no bare metal should protrude from the bottom of the cap. For an extra-secure connection, you can wrap the bottom of the nut to the wires with electric tape. One instance where you'd want to take this additional step might be if you need to cram several connections into an electrical box and a lot of maneuvering is necessary to make them all fit. Sometimes pushing wires around can loosen a connection and cause the wire to pull out of the cap—a definite no-no! Remember, it's crucial that you make good and secure contact with your wires when joining them in a wire nut. If you don't, you risk a having a nonfunctioning electrical item or, worse, creating a short.

Joining Solid-Core Wire

TOOLS
- Wire stripper
- Lineman's pliers
- Wire nut

1. Strip about an inch of insulation off the wire ends that you'll be joining.
2. Hold them side by side and begin twisting them together with lineman's pliers, turning clockwise at least two turns.
3. Snip the tip of the now-joined ends so they are even.
4. Place a wire nut over the ends and, turning clockwise, twist until tight.

Joining Stranded Wire

TOOLS
• Wire stripper

1. Strip about three-quarters of an inch of insulation off the wire ends that you'll be joining.
2. Inspect them to see that no wire strands have been accidentally cut off—if so, start over.
3. Gently twist each wire end with your forefinger and thumb to tighten the tip.
4. Hold them side by side and place a wire nut over the ends. Turning clockwise, twist until tight.

Chix Chat:

Four Girls and a Blackout

One night last summer, three girlfriends and I went into Manhattan for a special girls' night out. We booked a room at an ultraposh hotel and met there to have a cocktail and get dolled up before hitting the town. Well, you can imagine the scene: Dance music is blasting from the stereo, the TV's on too (even though no one's watching it), there are two blow dryers, a flat iron, *and* a curling iron all being used at the same time, and every single light fixture is on, because of course we need good light to do our makeup. We were

---

sucking enough electricity to power Rhode Island! I'm in the shower shampooing when—POP! The lights go out!

So there I am, just about to enter the rinse cycle, and it all goes black. This is followed by shrieks and cursing from my crazy friends (Brooklyn girls can pass from frightened to pissed off in about three seconds). They start yelling to me, "What the f@#$ do we do?!"

My girls know I'm the fix-it queen, but guess what? I'm naked, wet, and I have shampoo burning my eyes. "What the hell are you asking *me* for? I can't even find my way out of the bathtub!" Thank God someone had the brains to call the front desk. A half hour filled with the most intense giggling I can remember passed before they sent someone up to flip the circuit breaker and reprimand us for using every single outlet in the room simultaneously. Sorry, man.

CIRCUIT BREAKERS AND FUSES

Needing to reset a circuit breaker in a hotel room is as easy as picking up the phone, but what happens when you're home or someplace where there's no one to call?

Resetting a Circuit Breaker

A circuit breaker is designed to turn off, or "trip," the electricity when there's a short or overload in the circuit. If this happens, you will need to reset the circuit breaker. If all the steps on page 92 have been taken and your breaker keeps tripping, get on the horn with an electrician.

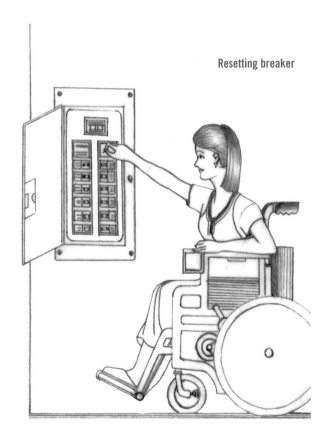

Resetting breaker

TOOLS
• Flashlight

1. Turn off and unplug whatever electrical items you were using before the lights went out.
2. Open your service panel (see "Safety Musts," page 86–87) and see which breaker switch—also called a toggle—is in the "off" position (some breakers trip to a middle or neutral position, rather than completely off). The tripped toggle will be the one in a different position from the others.
3. Flip that toggle all the way to the "off" position, then flip it to the "on" position.
4. Now go back and, one by one, plug in and turn on whatever electrical items you were using before the breaker tripped. If it trips again, you have overloaded the circuit and need to plug some of those items into a different circuit branch (see "Mapping Your Electric Utility," pages 84–85). Another possible cause for tripping a breaker may be that one of your electrical items is short-circuiting or overheating. Check each element for damaged or hot cords, smoke residue, or a burning odor.

Chix Tip: Update with Circuit Breakers

If problems with your fuses are making *you* blow a fuse, I suggest updating your service to a circuit-breaker system—it's safer and easier to live with. This project is not for a do-it-yourselfer. Call a licensed electrician.

Replacing a Fuse

Fuses, the grandmothers of the circuit breaker, are still found in older homes. If there's a problem, instead of tripping like a breaker, they blow, cutting off the electricity to that circuit branch. When this happens, the fuse must be replaced, so it's a good idea to keep extras on hand. You can purchase fuses in any hardware or electrical-supply store. The crucial information you need when purchasing replacement fuses is the correct amperage—this will be clearly indicated on the fuse. Amperage is the strength/amount of electric current and is measured in units called amperes, or amps for short. **Never replace an old fuse with a**

different-amp fuse—you risk causing an electrical fire. If all the steps below have been taken and your fuse keeps blowing, get on the horn with an electrician.

Plug-Type Fuse Replacement

Plug-type fuses are the most common. They are round with glass tops and come in different colors, which represent their amperage. They are available in 15, 20, 25, or 30 amps.

An S-type is a kind of plug fuse that comes with an adapter screwed onto its end. Once screwed into the socket, this adapter stays there, preventing a different-amp fuse from being screwed into it.

TOOLS
- Flashlight
- Replacement fuse

1. Turn off and unplug whatever electrical items you were using before the lights went out.
2. Open your service panel (see "Safety Musts," pages 86–87). Identify the blown fuse (it will be darkened in the center). A flashlight shone on the panel may help visibility.
3. Unscrew it and identify its amperage.
4. Screw in the new fuse, making sure to replace it with one of the same amperage.
5. Plug in and turn on whatever electrical

Various fuse types

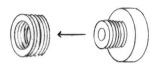

Plug-Style Fuse

S-Type Fuse
(prevents incorrect fuse ratings in service panel by adding nonremovable adapter)

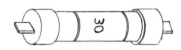

Cartridge-Style Fuse

Replacing a plug-type fuse

Chix Tip: Check if Your GFCI Is Tripped

If you have a power-out and all the breakers are in the "on" position and none of the fuses are blown, check your GFCI outlet and see if it has been tripped (see "Testing a Ground Fault Circuit Interrupter, page 103).

items you were using before the fuse blew, one by one. If the fuse blows again, you have overloaded the circuit and must plug one or more electrical items into a different circuit branch (see "Mapping Your Electric Utility," page 84). Another cause for blown fuses may be that a particular electrical item is short-circuiting or overheating. Check each article for damaged or hot cords, smoke residue, or a burning odor.

Cartridge-Type Fuse Replacement

TOOLS
- Fuse puller
- Multimeter
- Replacement fuse

1. Turn off and unplug whatever electrical items you were using before the lights went out.
2. Open your service panel (see "Safety Musts," pages 86–87). You cannot tell if a cartridge-type fuse is blown by looking at it, so check the map of your service panel (see "Mapping Your Electric Utility," page 84) to see which cartridge it could be.
3. With a fuse puller, extract the fuse by pulling from the center of the cartridge to release it from the clips. Never touch the metal ends of the fuse coming from the panel—they will be hot.
4. Test the fuse with a multimeter by touching each end with the probes and evaluate for "continuity." Continuity means there is a closed circuit—meaning electricity can flow. Set the multimeter to read "ohms Ω" (the measurement of resistance). If the multimeter gauge indicates low resistance, the fuse is still good. Test each cartridge until you find the one that has blown. Never test a cartridge while it's still in the service panel!
5. Replace the damaged fuse with an identical replacement. To best push the fuse back into the clips, plug it in by hand, not with the fuse puller.
6. Plug in and turn on whatever electrical items you were using

before the fuse blew, one by one. If the fuse blows again, you have overloaded the circuit and must plug one or more electrical items into a different circuit branch ("Mapping Your Electric Utility," page 84). Another cause for blown fuses may be that a particular electrical item is short-circuiting or overheating. Check each article for damaged or hot cords, smoke residue, or a burning odor.

SWITCHES AND OUTLETS

As my friend Susanna says, *"There is no such thing as ugly people, just bad lighting."*

Chix Chat:

Let There Be Light—the Right Light

Five P.M. In two hours the Boyfriend was arriving for the greatest night of his life—I was making him a home-cooked meal and was determined to have everything be perfect.

I've never subscribed to the old adage that "the way to a man's heart is through his stomach." Too often it backfires, and before you know it, you've traded all those romantic evenings out on the town for cozy meals at home—with *you* doing all the work. My girlfriend Lucia's mom always warned us, "Don't let a man know that you can cook," and believe me, we took this advice to heart.

But things were going so well with the Boyfriend that I thought it might be time to break my own rule and invite him to dinner. Now, when I cook, I really COOK. I pore over recipes, pair each course with the perfect wine, scour the farmers' market for the best of everything. Food, linens, silverware, crystal, flowers—you name it. Lucky dog, he didn't know what he was in for.

So by five-thirty, I'd sautéed, flambéed, organized, and arranged. I jumped into and out of the shower and was ready to transform myself from a frazzled sous-chef into a sultry goddess. Before dressing I took a moment to admire the beauty of the table setting. In the dining room, I had a gorgeous chandelier, adorned with cut crystals and scrolled brass, that had belonged to my grandmother. I flipped the switch and—YIKES! Blaring light! It was blinding! I should have put this chandelier in my bathroom! It was perfect for popping zits and tweezing extraneous facial hairs, but for a romantic dinner? Lord, no.

Picture it: me in my robe, hair in a towel, climbing up on top of the dining room table, dodging the glasses and china, trying to unscrew all these 20,000-watt bulbs. (Who in God's name bought them anyway?) But with half the bulbs gone, the lighting looked even worse. What was I going to do?

Fix it, of course!

I threw on sweats and jetted to my local hardware guy. I ran into the store ranting about dinner, lightbulbs, and whether or not I'd turned off the gas on my risotto. He looked at me like I was crazy, but that was nothing new. *Deep breath, Norma,* I told myself. I calmed down, and then out came two glorious words: "Dimmer switch."

Happily, a dimmer switch (or any switch, for that matter) takes only about five minutes to install. That left me a half hour to get gorgeous, throw on a Pavarotti CD, and greet the Boyfriend at the door with a glass of wine and the best damn lighting this side of Hollywood.

Replacing a Single-Pole Switch

Very simply, a switch puts a break in the flow of electrical current to an electrical item. This means that a standard switch is wired with only two black hot wires and a ground. The "on" position completes the contact of the hot wires, while the "off" breaks the contact. This type of switch has two terminals that the hot wires are connected to and is designated to one circuit (single pole). It doesn't matter which hot wire goes to which terminal—all that matters is the break in the connection.

When you open a switch box, you'll see white wires capped together and pushed to the back of the box. Just ignore them. These white neutral wires remain joined—again, a switch interrupts the flow of electricity in the black hot wires only.

There are many different types of switches that vary in style and function. There are three-way switches that control items from two locations, there are timers, pilot switches—the list goes on! In this project we're replacing the good ol' single-pole switch, which represents most switches in your home.

TOOLS
- Flathead or Phillips screwdriver
- Long-nose pliers
- Voltage indicator
- Replacement single-pole switch
- Electrical tape

1. Turn off the power at the service panel (review "Safety Musts," pages 86–87).

Single-pole switch

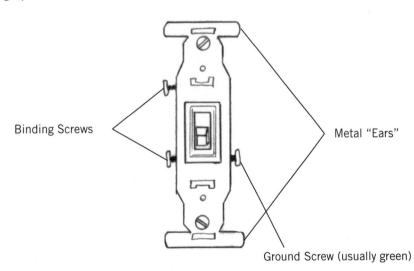

Binding Screws

Metal "Ears"

Ground Screw (usually green)

2. With a screwdriver, unscrew the plate cover and set it aside. Be careful not to lose the screws.

3. Unscrew the two screws in the metal "ears" and gently pull the switch out of the box.

4. Verify that the power is dead with a voltage indicator. Simply touch the probe to the terminals and see if it lights up—light indicates power. Never touch the terminals or wires until you are sure the power is off!

5. Loosen the terminal screws on the side of the outlet and unhook the wires. Or, if the wires are back wired (located in back of the switch), use a small flathead screwdriver to press inside the slot provided to "release" the wires. Unscrew the ground (if applicable), which will be a thin bare wire.

6. To attach the new switch, follow the same steps as above in reverse. Hook the wires back onto the terminals or reinsert the wires through the back if the switch is back-wired. Make sure the loop of the wire on a terminal hooks on in a clockwise direction, so it doesn't loosen as you tighten the screw over it. Be sure to orient the switch with the "off" label facing up and the toggle facing down (if applicable).

7. Wrap electrical tape around the switch to cover the screws on both sides.

8. Gently fold the wires back into the box, being careful not to disrupt any connections, and reattach the two screws through the metal ears. Screw back the plate cover.

9. With your new switch installed and plate cover on, restore power and turn it on. If it's not working, repeat steps 1–3 and recheck your connections.

Installing a Dimmer Switch

Changing a standard switch to a dimmer switch is a piece of cake. You'll probably spend more time picking one out than installing it! There are many colors and varieties of dimmers—rotary, slide, preset, et cetera.

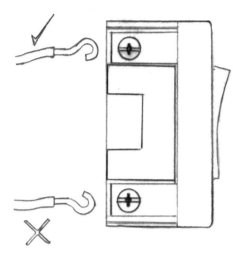

Wires should be bent in a clockwise direction
to prevent them from unhooking during tightening.

The one thing you have to make sure of is that you are replacing an ordinary single-pole switch with a single-pole dimmer.

A single-pole switch can be turned on in only one location. If a light can be turned on in two different locations, like at the top and the bottom of the stairs, it's called a three-way switch. I suggest tackling that project with a friend who has experience with three-way switches.

TOOLS
- Small flathead screwdriver or nail
- Wire stripper
- Phillips screwdriver
- Voltage indicator

1. Shut off the electricity at the main service panel (see "Safety Musts," pages 86–87).
2. With a screwdriver, remove the screws from the switchplate cover (don't lose those little suckers), then gently pull away the switch-

plate. You may need to persuade the cover off if it has been painted over—use a small screwdriver to pry it off.

3. Verify that the power is dead with a voltage indicator. Simply touch the probe to the terminals and see if it lights up—light indicates power. Never touch the terminals or wires until you are sure the power is off!

4. Now that the switch itself is exposed, with the Phillips head screwdriver, unscrew the top and bottom mounting screws and pull out the switch (you may have to tug on it).

5. Unhook the wires from the terminals by unscrewing them and slipping them off the terminal. Some switches may have the wires inserted in holes behind the switch. If that's the case, insert a nail or small screwdriver into the "release" slot next to each hole and pull the wires out. You'll see white wires capped together and pushed to the back of the electrical box— just ignore them. These white neutral wires remain joined—again, a switch interrupts the flow of electricity in the black hot wires only. In the event your old switch has a ground wire (a thin bare wire) screwed to it as well, unscrew it as you did the other two wires. The old switch will now be free—remove it.

6. To install your dimmer switch, first join the ground wire from the dimmer to the ground wire in the box (if there is a ground wire). Hold the exposed tips of the wires side by side, slip a wire nut over them, and turn it clockwise until it is tight. Then join the two wires from the dimmer to the wires coming out of the box (the two that were once joined to the old switch), using a wire nut. Make sure you have at least a half inch of wire for proper contact. To reveal more wire, pull off the insulation from your dimmer if it's precut or cut it off using a wire stripper (see "Wire: Cutting, Stripping, and Joining," page 88).

7. Gently fold the wires back into the box, being careful not to disrupt any connections, and then mount the dimmer with its screws. Make sure the dimmer is in the "off" position before restoring power.

Dimmer styles

Touch Control   Rotary   Slider

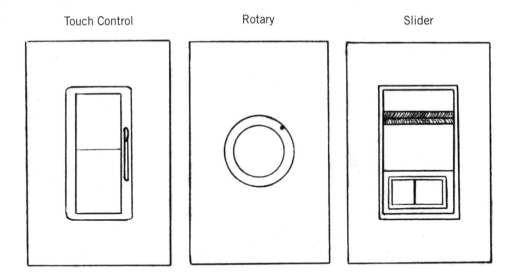

8. Turn on the power at the service panel. Verify that the dimmer is getting juice by using your voltage indicator or electricity tester. If it is, test the dimmer itself by turning the switch to the "on" position. In the event it doesn't work, turn off the power again and retrace your steps, making sure all your connections are tight. If it still doesn't work, call your favorite electrician!

9. Once you've verified that the dimmer is working, screw on your new plate cover and there you have it—lighting that's as bright or as dim, flattering, and romantic, as you like!

Replacing an Outlet

Whether you change an outlet for a new color or because it's just old and not functioning properly, replacing an outlet is an easy electric project. When choosing an outlet the most important element to be aware of is its amperage. Your new receptacle must have the same amp rating as the old one. Amperage will be clearly stamped in the plastic on the front of the outlet. FYI, typically, general-purpose outlets are rated 15 amp while small-appliance outlets are 20 amp.

TOOLS
- Circuit tester
- Flathead or Phillips screwdriver
- Long-nose pliers
- New replacement outlet
- Electrical tape

1. Shut off the power from the service panel (review "Safety Musts," pages 86–87).
2. Verify that the power is dead with a circuit tester. Simply plug it into the outlet and see if it lights up—light indicates power. Never touch the terminals or wires until you are sure the power is off.
3. Unscrew the plate cover to the outlet and set it aside. Don't lose the screw!
4. With a screwdriver, unscrew the two screws in the metal "ears" of the outlet and gently pull the outlet out of the box.
5. Your outlet will have either two or four wires attached to it—two if it's wired by itself or at the end of a circuit, four if it's in the middle of a circuit of outlets. There will be at least one black hot wire

Chix Tip:
Checking Out Outlets

There are several types of electricity testers. The most versatile and easy to use is a voltage indicator (see "Safety Musts," pages 86–87). However, for outlets, a circuit tester will not only let you know if the receptacle has power but also indicate if the outlet is grounded.

and one white neutral wire. There may also be a ground wire, which will be a thin bare wire.

6. With a screwdriver, loosen the terminal screws on the side of the outlet and unhook the wires. Or, if the wires come from the back of the outlet, use a small flathead screwdriver to press inside the slot provided to "release" the wires and pull them out. Unscrew the ground wire (if applicable).

7. To attach the new outlet, follow the same steps as above in reverse—hook the wires back onto the terminal screws or insert them in the back of the outlet. You may need to rebend the hook shape of the wire with pliers for a proper fit onto the terminal. Remember to connect the black and white wires to exactly the same terminals/holes as before. Hot wires go to the brass screws and neutral to silver, or, for holes, connect the wires to the holes on the corresponding brass and silver screw sides. Make sure the loop of the wire on a terminal hooks on in a clockwise direction, so it doesn't loosen as you tighten the screw over it.

8. Wrap electrical tape around the outlet to cover the screws on both sides.

9. Fold the wires back into the box, being careful not to disrupt any connections while doing so.

10. With your new outlet installed and plate cover on, restore power and test with the circuit tester. If the outlet isn't working, repeat above steps 1–3 and recheck your connections.

Testing a Ground Fault Circuit Interrupter (GFCI)

A GFCI (ground fault circuit interrupter) is a type of outlet designed to detect a variance in the incoming and outgoing current in an outlet, caused by an electrical leak. When this "ground fault" occurs, the GFCI will interrupt the current, tripping the outlet, thus killing the power in a fraction of a second. Basically, it's an outlet with its own built-in circuit breaker. A GFCI will have a black "test" and a red "reset" button on the face of it. When it trips, the reset button pops out. In order for electricity to flow again, you need to press the reset button. A GFCI will kill power

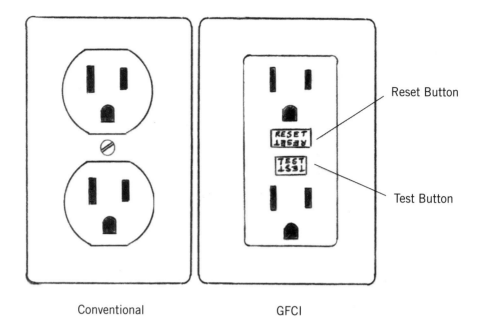

Reset Button

Test Button

Conventional   GFCI

to any outlets "downstream" from it — in other words, any outlet that is wired in a series after the GFCI will also lose current.

Electrical code today requires that GFCIs be installed in any "damp" area of your home, like a kitchen, bathroom, or basement. If your home doesn't have GFCIs in areas where there is water, I strongly suggest installing them. You should test the GFCI after installation and every few months thereafter to make sure it is working properly.

TOOLS
• Lamp

1. Plug a lamp into the GFCI outlet and turn it on.
2. Press the test button. This should trip the outlet, making the reset button pop out, killing the power, and shutting off the lamp. If it doesn't, either there is faulty wiring or the interrupter mechanism is no longer functioning. If this is the case, you will need to replace the outlet.

Installing a GFCI

Wiring a GFCI is similar to wiring a regular outlet, with one difference: The back of the GFCI outlet is marked with terminals "line" and "load."

BEFORE YOU START THIS PROJECT, YOU MUST READ THE FOLLOWING:

DETERMINING INCOMING AND OUTGOING WIRES

If you open your outlet and find four wires (plus two grounds), you must determine which are the incoming and which are the outgoing. **Incoming and outgoing** wires describe which wires are coming from the service panel (incoming) and which continue to supply electricity to other receptacles in a series (outgoing).

To make this determination, kill the power at the service panel, then separate all four wires and wire-nut each of them. Turn the power on. ONE PAIR OF THESE WIRES WILL NOW BE LIVE. Carefully remove the wire nuts off one pair of black and white wires and test them with a voltage indicator.

REMEMBER—TWO OF THESE WIRES WILL BE LIVE.

DO NOT LET THESE WIRES TOUCH ANYTHING BUT THE TESTER PROBES. IT IS SAFE TO HANDLE THE WIRE BY THE PLASTIC SHEATHING, BUT DO NOT TOUCH THE EXPOSED TIP.

The pair that indicates incoming current always connects to the "line" terminals. Now you know that the other pair is outgoing and therefore connects to the "load" terminals.

TOOLS
- Flathead or Phillips screwdriver
- Long-nose pliers
- Circuit tester
- New replacement outlet
- Electrical tape
- 4" length of ground wire (if applicable)
- Wire nut (if applicable)
- Ground jumper

Rear View of GFCI Receptacle

Additional items
you want protected
by the GFCI
MUST be connected
to the LOAD screws

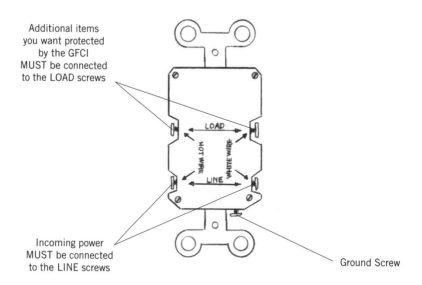

Incoming power
MUST be connected
to the LINE screws

Ground Screw

1. To remove the old outlet, shut the power from the service panel (review "Safety Musts," pages 86–87).

2. Verify that the power is dead with a circuit tester. Simply plug it into the outlet and see if it lights up — light indicates power. Never touch the terminals or wires until you are sure the power is off.

3. With a screwdriver, unscrew the plate cover to the outlet and set it aside. Don't lose the screw!

4. With a screwdriver, unscrew the two screws in the metal "ears" of the outlet and gently pull the outlet out of the box.

5. Your outlet will have either two or four wires attached to it — two if it's wired by itself or at the end of a circuit, four if it's in the middle of a circuit of outlets. There will be at least one black hot wire and one white neutral wire. There may also be a ground wire, which will be a thin bare wire.

6. With a screwdriver, loosen the terminal screws on the side of the outlet and unhook the wires. Or, if the wires come from the back of the outlet, use a small flathead screwdriver to press inside the slot provided to "release" the wires and pull them out. Unscrew the ground wire (if applicable).

7. To install the GFCI, if there's one set of black and white wires, attach these incoming wires (originating from the service panel) to the terminals labeled "line." You may need to rebend the "hook" shape of the wire with pliers for a proper fit onto the terminal.

8. In the event that there are two sets of wires, see "Determining Incoming and Outgoing Wires" page 105. Attach the outgoing black and white wires (that lead to other receptacles in a series) to the terminals labeled "load."

9. Connect grounds with a ground jumper and wire nut. (A ground jumper is a piece of ground wire that "jumps" from the outlet to join the other grounds and connects them all together with a wire nut.)

10. Turn power back on at the service panel and test the GFCI (see "Testing a Ground Fault Circuit Interrupter," page 103).

LIGHTS

The right light fixture can make a room go from dud to dazzling. Once you learn how easy it is to replace one, don't be surprised if you want to change fixtures all over your house!

Replacing a Light Fixture

TOOLS
- Ladder or stepstool
- Flathead or Phillips screwdriver
- Voltage indicator
- Wire nuts (should come with the fixture)
- Electrical tape (optional, to reinforce wire nuts)
- Hammer (you never know)

Light fixture

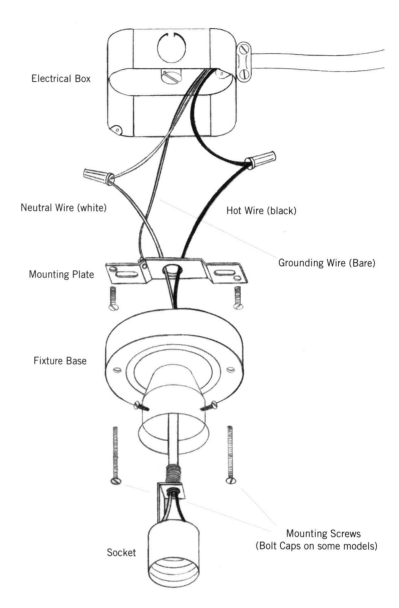

Electrical Box

Neutral Wire (white)

Hot Wire (black)

Grounding Wire (Bare)

Mounting Plate

Fixture Base

Socket

Mounting Screws
(Bolt Caps on some models)

- Wire strippers (ditto)
- Pliers (ditto)
- Adjustable wrench (ditto)
- Wire hanger
- Safety glasses (if you'll be working over your head on a ceiling fixture)

1. Kill the power at the service panel (see "Safety Musts," pages 86–87).

2. Climb a ladder or stepstool to remove the existing fixture. There are two common ways it will be mounted. One type of fixture has two fine threaded bolts that are spaced about four inches apart. Unscrew the bolt caps by hand, then pull and slightly twist the fixture toward the open end of the bolts. The light will then drop free. (If the fixture is stuck in place with paint, gently tap it or pry it loose with a flat screwdriver.) The other type of mounting, commonly found in chandeliers, is held in place with a single cap nut in the center of the fixture. Simply unscrew it. Only the electrical wires actually come through the center of the nut, so be sure not to twist them when you unscrew this type of fixture. Once the screws are out, be prepared to support the weight of it. Do not let it dangle from the wires!

3. Unscrew the wire nuts to disconnect the old fixture. Verify that the power is dead with a voltage indicator. Simply touch the probe to the wires and see if it lights up—light indicates power. Never touch the wires until you are sure the power is off. One black, one white, and one ground wire (depending on how the old fixture was grounded) will remain. Make sure the ends of the wires are not damaged or frayed for a proper connection to your new fixture (see "Wire: Cutting, Stripping, and Joining, page 88). Also, remember how the old fixture was grounded, as you'll reground the new fixture the same way.

4. Determine if the new mount is the same as the old one. If it is different, you will have to install a piece or two of new hardware. This may include a strap or a center-mounted, hollow-threaded bolt called a nipple. (Look at the instructions that come with your light fixture to help guide you—you may not need all the parts that come with the fixture.)

5. Installing a light fixture is a balancing act—you have to make the connections while holding the fixture in place. Temporarily hang the fixture from the strap while you work with a bent piece of wire

hanger (having the wire act as a hook) or have a friend hold it for you while you make the connections. Again, do not let the fixture dangle by the electric wires!

6. Use the wire nuts provided in the light kit and attach the wires—white to white, black to black, and green wire to the bare ground wire or directly to the metal electrical box (ground the new fixture according to how your old fixture was grounded). It is important to ground the fixture, so don't skip this step.

7. Once all of the wiring is secure, fold the wires back into the box, being careful not to disrupt any connections while doing so. Slide the light into place over the mounting bolts and screw on the bolt caps. (If you are installing a fixture, such as a chandelier, where the wires exit through the center nut, be careful not to twist the wires as you secure the nut.)

8. Install the bulb(s) in the light. Remember not to exceed the maximum wattage listed on the sockets. This is a fire hazard.

9. Turn the power back on from the service panel and test the light.

10. If everything looks okay, turn the light off and install the globe, shades, or other decorative trim. If you're installing a globe, make sure that its retaining screws are snug, but be careful not to over-tighten them, or you risk breaking the glass.

CEILING FANS

I have an image in my mind of the perfect room, a room I've been fantasizing about my whole life. I always picture this grand room in a luxurious house tucked away on a tropical island, with big French doors all the way around. Sunlight streaming through white muslin drapery, dark wooden British Colonial furniture, oversize silk couches, eclectic island treasures adorning the end tables, exotic plants in full bloom at each corner—and best of all? In the center of the room, a ceiling fan with blades of carved bamboo, gently spinning a cool tropical breeze . . . Okay, that's the dream, this is the reality: a ground-floor apartment in noisy, freezing-cold New York City. But even if I can't have the island, the ceiling fan? No problem.

A ceiling fan is both attractive and functional. It can provide light, cool or warm a space, and embellish the look of any room in your house. When choosing a fan, there's more to consider than just looks (good advice when you're choosing a guy, too!). One of the most important things to take into account is blade clearance. Ideally, you should have a minimum of 12 inches above the fan blades for proper air circulation. Although some fans can be installed with a flush mount for low-ceilinged rooms, this drastically reduces their effectiveness. You *must* have at least 7 feet under the blades, or you risk taking off the top of a tall friend's head. A minimum of 18 inches from the blade tips to the wall is also advised.

Many fans have a reverse switch, which is great in the winter. Since heated air rises, it's always warmer near the ceiling. Running the fan in reverse forces the cooler air up and the warm air down, mixing it, so your room will be more evenly heated.

If you already have a light fixture in the proper location, it couldn't be easier to replace it with a ceiling fan. If you don't have a ceiling fixture, you should hire an electrician to run power to the spot you want to hang your ceiling fan.

If you have an existing fixture box in the ceiling, it is important to determine its sturdiness before hanging a fan from it. To safely hang a ceiling fan, the fixture must be anchored either directly to a ceiling joist (a wooden beam), or to a sturdy cross brace mounted across the box. Once you remove the existing light fixture, examine how the box is mounted in the ceiling. There should be a little space between the box

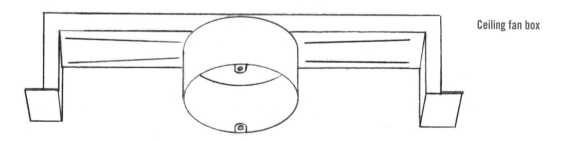

Ceiling fan box

and the drywall—shine a flashlight over the box. If the gap isn't wide enough, slide a small screwdriver into the slot and gently poke around, feeling for the joist or brace. If there is a solid brace over the box, you should be able to tell pretty easily.

The most frustrating thing about installing a fan is losing some of the small parts that come with it in several tiny bags. Your impulse will be to cut open all of the bags and dump everything out—don't! Read the directions, work step-by-step, and open only what you need when you need it. (Incidentally, you won't need everything that comes packaged with the fan, since the manufacturer provides enough hardware for more than one potential installation scenario.)

Hanging a Ceiling Fan

TOOLS
- New ceiling fan and kit
- Flathead or Phillips screwdriver
- Voltage tester
- Wire nuts (should come with the fan)
- Wire stripper
- Pliers (you never know)
- Adjustable wrench (ditto)
- Ladder
- Safety glasses (always wear them when working above your head)

1. Kill the power from the service panel (see "Safety Musts," pages 86-87).
2. Remove the existing fixture (see "Replacing a Light Fixture," page 107).
3. Establish that the ceiling box is suitably braced (as described above).
4. Attach the mounting bracket for the new fan to the ceiling box with the screws provided or with the existing screws if they fit. If your ceiling is vaulted, make sure when placing the bracket into position that the open side of the bracket is facing the high side. You will see why in step 6.

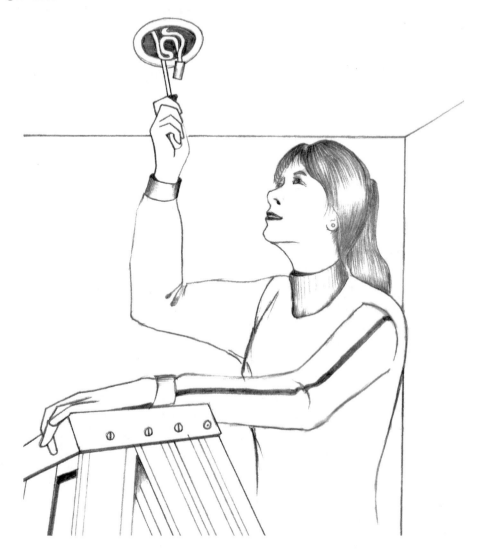

5. There is some minor assembly required to prepare the fan motor for installation. Look at the parts and the instructions that have been provided. If you have a high ceiling and your fan has a down rod, you will have to thread the fan's power wires through it and

insert it into the top of the motor. The rod is usually secured with a pin and cotter key. A hanger ball fits over the other end of the rod and is secured with a similar pin. Last, the trim shroud must be loaded onto the rod at this time. Be sure to review your fan's assembly diagram carefully, since it may vary from this description and the order of assembly is critical for construction.

6. Once the hanging assembly is ready, you can lift the fan into place and drop the hanging ball into the hanger bracket. You will need a ladder and maybe a friend to hand up the motor assembly. Often there is a groove in the plastic ball that fits into a key on the hanger bracket. The hanger is shaped like a ball so the fan can hang plumb even if you have an angled ceiling. On a steeply vaulted ceiling, because of the angle, the ball could potentially slip out if you installed the open side of the bracket facing down in step 4. Once in place, the bracket will hold the weight of the fan, so you can let go.

7. With the weight of the fan supported, you can easily make the wiring connections. Use the wire nuts provided in the fan kit and attach the wires white to white, black to black, and green to bare, or directly to the metal box (see "Replacing a Light Fixture," page 107). It is important to ground the fixture, so don't skip this step. Also, if there is an additional black or blue wire, it is likely for an optional light kit. Attach this wire to the black ones, even if you don't have a light for your fan. You may decide to add one later, and this will save you a step.

8. Once all of the wiring is secure, fold the wires back into the box, being careful not to disrupt any connections while doing so. Slide the wiring shroud up against the ceiling and screw it into place. If you have a light kit, follow the mounting directions listed with the fan.

9. The only thing left now is the attachment of the blades. Using the bolts and washers provided, attach the brackets to the blades while you're still down on the floor and then cart them up the ladder and

screw them to the fan motor. Make sure that these screws are snug.

10. Turn the power back on from the service panel.

11. Test the fan. If it doesn't come on when you hit the wall switch, check the pull chain. Most fans have a chain that controls the various speeds and a switch to reverse the direction of the blades. Be sure to bring the fan to a complete stop before reversing its direction. Changing the direction while the fan is turning may cause damage.

12. If your fan wobbles, check to make sure that it is hanging plumb and that it is solidly seated in the hanger bracket. If the shaking persists, get an inexpensive fan-balancing kit and follow the simple directions to solve the problem. It's well worth the effort to eliminate the annoying and potentially damaging vibration. If you just can't cure the wobble, take the fan back and get a replacement. Some are just built broken.

DOORBELLS

When your doorbell's "ding-dong" goes dud, what do you do? Fix it or replace the ding-dang thing! There are three main parts in your doorbell's anatomy:

- the button (which often cracks if it's plastic)
- the bell or chimes
- the transformer

These components are initially powered from the service panel, then wired through the transformer, then through a circuit that loops from the button to the bell and back to the transformer. The button acts like a switch—when it's depressed, it closes the circuit and the bell rings.

The wire to your doorbell will probably be 18 or 20 gauge—they're very skinny. These are low-voltage lines and can't shock you. At the most they'll give you a little tingle, but I still recommend that you shut down the power to the bell (at the service panel) until you confirm the low-voltage wires.

Doorbell circuits

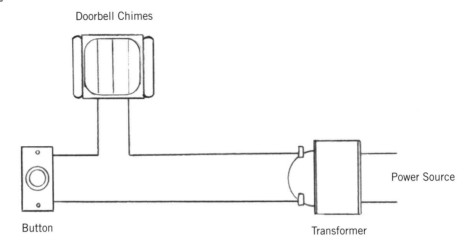

Doorbell Chimes

Power Source

Button

Transformer

Doorbell Replacement

If the bell still works and you just want to change the button because it's cracked or ugly, the replacement is easy.

TOOLS
- New button
- Phillips or flathead screwdriver
- Voltage indicator

1. Shut the power to the existing bell from the service panel (see "Safety Musts," pages 86–87).
2. Unscrew the top and bottom screws on the housing of the button and pull it out to expose the wires.
3. Verify that the power is dead with a voltage indicator. Simply touch the probe to the wires and see if it lights up—light indicates power. Never touch the terminals or wires until you are sure the power is off. (Even though doorbell wiring is usually low-voltage and won't give you a shock, I still recommend this safety step.)
4. Unhook the wires attached to the back of the button.

5. Connect the wires to the back of your new button—wrap them around the terminal screw clockwise, the same direction in which you'll be tightening those screws.

6. Gently fold the wires back behind the button and press it up to the wall.

7. Screw the top and bottom mounting screws of your new button back into the wall.

Chix Tricks: A New Use for Toothpicks

If the holes in the wall are too wide to hold the new screws, stick toothpicks in the hole. Squeeze in some wood glue and break off the tips so they're flush with the wall. This will add new wood to screw the new button mounting into.

Testing Your Doorbell Wiring

If your doorbell just isn't working, run these checks on the button.

TOOLS
- Phillips or flathead screwdriver
- Voltage indicator
- Wire stripper
- Wire brush

1. Shut the power to the bell from the service panel.

2. Unscrew the top and bottom screws on the housing of the button and pull it out to expose the wires.

3. Verify that the power is dead with a voltage indicator. Simply touch the probe to the wires and see if it lights up—light indicates power. Never touch the terminals or wires until you are sure the power is off.

4. Unhook the wires attached to the back of the button. Identify that they are low-voltage by the thinness of the gauge. If the wires to your doorbell aren't low-voltage, close the bell up and call a professional—the follwing steps require checking live wires in a situation that is appropriate only for a trained professional.

5. Once low voltage is determined, turn the power back on at the service panel. Back at the door, touch the two wires of the bell together. This should make the bell sound.

6. If it doesn't, check that the wires are in good shape. With wire stripper strip the tips to make clean wire ends (see "Wire: Cutting, Stripping, and Joining," page 88). Touch the wires to each other again to see if they make the bell ring.

7. Check that the terminals on the button are clean, for good contact. Brush them clean. Reattach the wires to the terminals and test the button. If the bell is still not working, it could be faulty wiring elsewhere, like at the transformer, or a malfunction at the bell/chime unit itself.

Checking the Transformer

A transformer reduces 110 volts from the service panel down to approximately 20 volts to the doorbell. This low voltage is why doorbell wiring is a very thin gauge. The great news is that this low voltage cannot shock you.

TOOLS
• Multimeter
• Phillips or flathead screwdriver

1. Locate the transformer. It's usually near the service panel, the hot-water tank, or the door itself.

2. Disconnect the bell's wires from the transformer. Touch the probes of a multimeter to the terminals. If no voltage is registered on the meter, you'll need to replace the transformer.

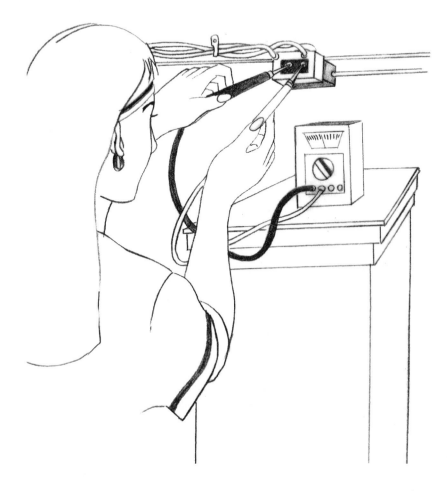

3. Shut off the power to the bell from the service panel (see "Safety Musts," pages 86–87).

4. Verify that the power is dead with a voltage indicator. Simply touch the probe to the wires and see if it lights up—light indicates power. Never touch the terminals or wires until you are

sure the power is off! Be advised: Lines to the transformer from the service panel will *not* be low-voltage; they will be 110 volts.

5. Disconnect the 110-volt lines powering the transformer and dismount it.

6. Bring the old transformer to the hardware store for an exact replacement.

7. Remount the new transformer. Reconnect both the power lines and the bell wires.

8. Turn the power back on and test the bell.

Checking the Bell or Chimes

If the transformer and wiring have been checked and are working properly, the culprit may be the bell or chimes.

TOOLS
- Phillips or flathead screwdriver
- Wire brush

1. Shut off the power to the bell from the service panel (see "Safety Musts," pages 86–87).

2. Disconnect the bell or chimes and check that the terminals are clean for good contact. Wire-brush them clean.

3. Reconnect the bell/chime, turn the power back on, and test the bell.

4. If the bell/chime unit still isn't working, you may want to replace it. By this point you'll practically be a doorbell pro—it will be easy to disconnect and dismount the old bell/chime unit and replace it with a new one. There will be just two wires and mounting screws. Bring your old bell/chime unit to your hardware store and replace it with one that is compatible with your doorbell setup. Mount the new bell/chime with the screws provided and reconnect the wires.

5. Turn the power back on and test the bell.

If your doorbell isn't working and you've tested all the components as described in the projects above, you may have faulty wiring somewhere behind your walls. At this point you have three reasonable choices:

- Call a professional.
- Install one of the new remote doorbells — they work on radio waves and are wireless. Hallelujah.
- Do it the old-fashioned way — mount a knocker!

Walls and Floors

WALLS AND FLOORS BASIX: KEEPING THEIR STRUCTURE STABLE AND STUNNING

When I'm learning something for the first time, I always try to relate it to something I'm already familiar with—like cooking, shoe shopping, and searching for that magic wrinkle cream. Thinking in terms I already understand makes it easier to master the new task. I know I'm not the only one out there who thinks this way. When I teach other women about home improvement, I find that they're more comfortable if I explain projects in ways that they can relate to. If I'm describing how to apply adhesive to the back of a tile, I'll say, "Spread it on like you're icing a cupcake."

Or if I'm explaining how wood swells in certain weather conditions, I'll relate it to how we bloat after eating five pounds of olive spread on crusty Italian bread. People laugh when I make wacky analogies, but it's through humor and familiarity that we get comfortable with terms like mastic (tile glue) and hygroscopic behavior (how wood, for example, swells and shrinks).

Having a weakness for analogies (and olive spread), I'd like to really indulge myself in the projects involving the part of the house that we literally see and touch—our walls and floors. A home is a living, breathing structure. The plumbing in a home is a body's blood supply—water, like blood, brings life. Electricity is our central nervous system. It sends charged current throughout our home that feeds impulses on command.

But the walls and floors are our skin. They're what we and everyone else are looking at day after day. They hold in all our pipes and wires, protect us from the elements, and make us look old and saggy when they're not properly cared for. This next section has fixes to keep our walls and floors healthy, strong, and looking fabulous. (With that in mind, I'd better go book a facial.)

DRYWALL AND PLASTER ANATOMIES AND REMEDIES

Drywall, gypsum board, wallboard, Sheetrock, "rock"—different names, same thing—is the material that comprises most walls. Gypsum is a naturally occurring mineral and is the primary ingredient in wallboard. It is ground down from its rocklike state and sandwiched between two tough pieces of paper, creating sheets of drywall. The majority of homes today have "rock" walls. In the past, walls were made of strips of wood (lath), with plaster troweled over them, creating a smooth surface known as plaster walls.

Telling the difference between drywall and plaster is not difficult. If your home was built pre–World War II your walls are plaster. If you're not sure of the date of your home, the easiest way to check is by knocking—Sheetrock walls are hollow sounding, whereas plaster walls make a *thud* sound when you rap them. Still not sure? Take a small nail and with a hammer tap it in an inconspicuous spot on the wall. If the nail drives straight through easily, it's drywall.

DRYWALL REPAIRS

My grandfather used to say, "There's more than one way to skin a cat." I always thought that was a pretty sick expression, especially since I'm a cat lover. Nonetheless, it still makes the valuable point that there are many different ways to get a job done.

This certainly holds true for wall repair. If you get a room filled with fifty construction pros, they'll each have their own version of how to do a patch. But you can count on one constant: Each one is adamant that he (or she) alone knows the best way to get the job done. The repairs I list below are *my* way (the right way).

Repairing Cracks in Drywall

TOOLS

- Newspaper
- 2-inch putty knife
- Rag
- Joint compound
- Dust mask
- Medium-grit sanding block
- Spray elastic crack sealant
- Primer and paint

1. Place newspaper on the floor under the crack to protect your floors from dripping joint compound and plaster particles.

2. With the corner tip of the putty knife, clean out any loose drywall from the crack. You should slightly open up very fine cracks to be sure they're wide enough to get filled—but don't overdo it and make more work for yourself. Wipe the crack down with a rag to make sure that it's all cleaned out.

3. Load the putty knife with joint compound. Approximate the amount by the size of the crack. With the putty knife held at approximately a forty-five-degree angle to the wall, press the compound into the crack, beginning at the top. Run the knife down along the length of the crack, pressing in the compound as you go. Be sure that the entire crack is filled, so reload your knife and go over it if necessary. It is normal for excess plaster to spread beyond the edges of the crack.

Cleaning loose drywall with putty knife

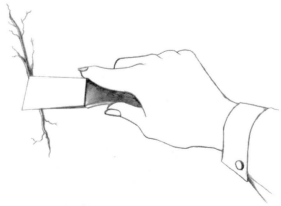

Sanding edges of patch

4. Allow the patch to dry for several hours. Once it's all white and powdery, you can sand it, being sure to smooth the edges where the patch meets the wall surface. Wear a mask when sanding. Wipe the patch with a rag to clean off the dust.

5. Check to see if the joint compound has shrunk after drying and left indentations. If this is the case, the patch will need another layer of compound (repeat steps 3–4).

6. Spray an elastic crack sealant over the patch, following product directions.

7. Paint the repair with a primer or your matching flat wall color. If your wall has a shine to its paint finish, like eggshell or semigloss, you must give it a coat of primer or flat paint first. Paint that has a shine to its finish will always "flash" directly over a patch, which means it will leave a visible difference in finish compared to the rest of the wall, unless you prime it first.

Repairing Small Holes in Drywall

Use this repair only if the hole in your wall is smaller than a couple of inches in diameter.

TOOLS
- Newspaper
- 2-inch putty knife

- Rag
- Joint compound
- Dust mask
- Medium-grit sanding block
- Primer and paint

1. Place newspaper on the floor under the hole to protect your floors from dripping joint compound and plaster particles.
2. With the corner tip of the putty knife, clean out any loose drywall from the hole. Wipe it down with a rag to make sure that it's all cleaned out of the hole.
3. Load the putty knife with joint compound. Approximate the amount by the size of the hole. With the putty knife held at approximately a forty-five-degree angle to the wall, press the compound into the hole while passing the blade diagonally from left to right along the surface of the hole and wall. Be sure that the entire crack is filled, so go over it if you must. It is normal for excess plaster to spread beyond the edges of the hole.
4. Allow the patch to dry for several hours. Once the compound is all white and powdery, sand it, being sure to smooth the edges where the patch meets the wall surface. Wear a dust mask when sanding. Wipe the patch with a rag to clean off the dust.

Pressing compound into hole

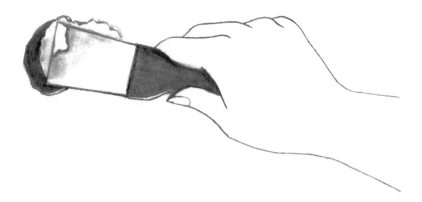

5. Check to see if the joint compound has shrunk, leaving indentations that aren't flush with the wall. If this is the case, the patch will need another layer of compound. Repeat steps 3–4, only this time pass the blade diagonally from right to left (this will fill in misses from the opposite direction—it works great).

6. Paint the repair with a primer or your matching flat wall color. If your wall has a shine to its paint finish, like eggshell or semigloss, you must give it a coat of primer or flat paint first. Paint that has a shine to its finish will always "flash" directly over a patch, which means it will leave a visible difference in finish compared to the rest of the wall, unless you prime it first.

Repairing Medium to Large Holes

Use this repair only if the hole in your wall is larger than a couple of inches in diameter. This type of patch has several names—hot patch, blow patch, hat patch, Dutchman, to name a few.

TOOLS
- Newspaper
- Drywall saw
- Tape measure
- Scrap piece of drywall (the same thickness as your existing wall—usually $\frac{1}{2}$ inch, but measure or bring a sample broken out of the hole to your home center)
- Utility knife
- Spray bottle with water
- 4-inch putty knife
- Joint compound
- Dust mask
- Medium-grit sanding block
- Rag
- Primer and paint

Squaring the hole

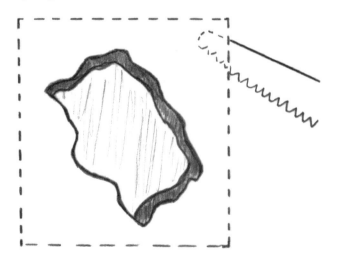

1. Place newspaper on the floor under the hole to protect your floor from splattering joint compound and plaster particles.

2. With the drywall saw, clean the edges of your hole by cutting out a square around it.

3. Use a tape measure to take a measurement of the now-square hole.

4. With your drywall saw, cut out a piece from your scrap that is 2 inches wider than your square.

5. Set the repair piece facedown, on the white paper side (the back side of the paper is grayish in color). Use a utility knife to score the dimensions of your hole on the back side of the repair piece—this will leave a two-inch "brim." Now follow your scored lines and continue to cut through the "rock" of the drywall with the utility knife, being careful to preserve the front of the paper—you're going to need that, so do not cut all the way through.

6. Snap the cut edges off the repair piece and peel the "rock" off the front side of the paper. You should be left with a repair piece the size of your hole that has a 2-inch paper brim around it.

7. Plug the patch into the hole to dry-test the fit. Use a utility knife to shave the edges of the "rock" if it's too big.

8. Take the repair piece out of the hole and spray the edges around the hole with water; then do the same to the back side of the paper brim.

9. Load your putty knife with joint compound and butter the edges of the hole, then the back side of the paper brim, with a generous amount of compound (approximately a $\frac{3}{8}$-inch layer).

Chix Tip: The Joys of Joint Compound

Joint compound, also referred to as mud, is a product that is spread over the seams, or "joints," where sheets of wallboard meet. It is also used to fill and repair dimples, cracks, and holes in walls. Vinyl spackle (or spackling) is similar to joint compound but it dries faster and is typically used for smaller repairs. I prefer having a tub of premixed all-purpose joint compound on hand (as opposed to the powdered type you have to mix yourself): With it I'm ready for any size patch. It's applied to a wall surface with a putty knife, or for bigger areas, it's spread on with a trowel. Be sure to keep the lid of the joint compound bucket on tight so the product doesn't dry out.

Paper Layers

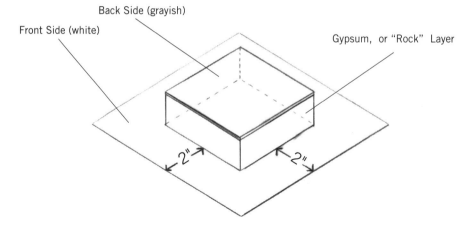

Preparing a 2-Inch Paper Brim Around Patch

10. Plug the patch into the hole, pressing down the brim and squishing down the joint compound.
11. With the putty knife held at approximately a forty-five-degree angle to the wall, smooth down the edges of the patch, removing excess compound. (As you're working, drop the excess compound back in its container for reuse.) The paper brim should be flat on the wall surface and covered with a thin coat of compound.
12. Allow the patch to dry for several hours.
13. Once it's all white and powdery, you can sand it, being sure to smooth the edges where the patch meets the wall surface. Wear a dust mask when sanding. Wipe the patch with a rag to clean off the dust.
14. Paint the repair with a primer or your matching flat wall color. If your wall has a shine to its paint finish, like eggshell or semigloss, you must give it a coat of primer or flat paint first. Paint that has a shine to its finish will always "flash" directly over a patch, which means it will leave a visible difference in finish compared to the rest of the wall, unless you prime it first.

Holy Mama, That Hole Is HUGE Hole Repair!

This patch is for a hole you can stick a microwave in!

TOOLS
- Newspaper
- Drywall saw
- Tape measure
- Scrap piece of drywall (the same thickness as your existing wall)
- 1x3-inch wood lengths (quantity will depend on the size of your patch)
- Wood handsaw
- Several 1-inch coarse drywall screws
- Drill or power driver
- Utility knife
- Nylon mesh drywall tape
- 4-inch putty knife
- Joint compound
- Dust mask
- Medium-grit sanding block
- Rag
- Primer and paint

1. Place newspaper on the floor under the hole to protect your floor from splattering joint compound and plaster particles.
2. With the drywall saw, cut around the damaged drywall, making a clean square shape.
3. Use a tape measure to take the measurement of the now-square hole and cut the scrap drywall to the same dimensions.
4. Using these measurements, configure and cut your 1x3s with a wood handsaw so that they are the correct size to frame the inside of the hole. You are going to screw these in place along the inside edges of your square hole so that you can screw the drywall patch to them.
5. Place a 1x3 on the inside of one edge, leaving half of the wood's width exposed and the other half behind the wall. Screw it in place, driving through the wall with the drywall screws. Repeat this

1x3 inside hole

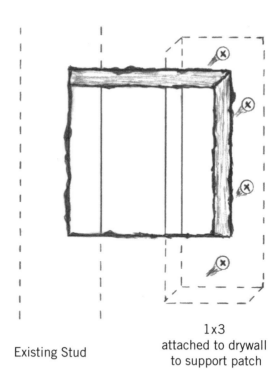

Existing Stud

1x3
attached to drywall
to support patch

process on all four sides, unless your patch is next to an existing stud. In that case, use your utility knife to cut through the drywall, exposing half of the stud so that one side of your hole is bordered with half a stud and the other is bordered with your 1x3.

6. With your hole framed, test-fit the repair piece. Use a utility knife to shave the edges if it's too big.

7. Screw the repair piece onto the framing, putting at least two screws in each side.

8. Tape each joint with the mesh drywall tape. This tape will self-adhere to the wall.

9. Load the putty knife with a small fistful-size amount of joint compound. Holding the knife at approximately a forty-five-degree angle to the wall, press the compound along the joints, being sure to cover the tape and smooth out the edges.

10. Allow the patch to dry for several hours.

11. If any tape is still exposed, spread another layer of compound and allow it to dry.

12. Once the compound is all white and powdery, you can sand it. Be sure to smooth the edges where the patch meets the wall surface. Wear a dust mask when sanding. Wipe the patch with a rag to clean off the dust.

13. Paint the repair with a primer or your matching flat wall color. If your wall has a shine to its paint finish, like eggshell or semigloss, you must give it a coat of primer or flat paint first. Paint that has a shine to its finish will always "flash" directly over a patch, which means it will leave a visible difference in finish compared to the rest of the wall, unless you prime it first.

Applying mesh drywall tape

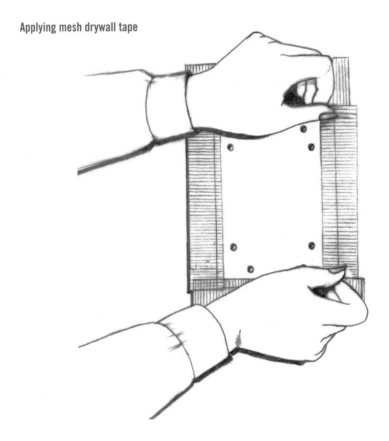

Chix Tip:
Your Power Drill Is Your Friend

Yes, your girlfriend can stay up all night with you and listen to you kvetch about the lack of good guys in the dating pool and pass you tissues as you share all the ugly details of yet another failed blind date. But can she drive screws, bore holes, and make assembling the standing shelves you ordered a breeze instead of a frustrating fiasco producing blistered and bloody hands and culminating in the erection of something that looks like the leaning tower of Pisa?

The first power tool anyone should own is a drill. It is the absolute must-have when it comes to getting into the nitty-gritty of home improvement.

There are several different types of drills—cordless, hammer, impact—each possessing various features: chuckless, cordless, varying volts, speeds, and clutches. (*Oy vey*—the list goes on! We could spend days on the pros and cons of each, but let me save you the mind meld and recommend my drill of choice—a 12 volt cordless power drill/driver.

This drill runs on a battery pack that has plenty of driving power but is not excessively heavy (as are drills with higher voltage and larger batteries). It has a keyless "chuck" (the tip of the drill that holds the bit), which means you don't need a "key" to open and close the chuck when changing bits. As with most any drill, this one can hold a Phillips head bit, square drive, wood, metal, or masonry bits, hole saw bits, a bit extender, etc. As long as the shank of the bit does not exceed the maximum chuck opening (which will be either $\frac{3}{8}$ or $\frac{1}{2}$ in diameter). Be sure to check the shank shape and diameter when purchasing bits to be sure they will fit your drill.

Here's how to operate a cordless drill/driver:

- Read the operating/safety instructions and follow procedures for charging the battery. Observe all safety warnings. Every drill is slightly different, so familiarize yourself with all the parts.
- **To insert a bit:** Hold the chuck collar (the stationary part of the chuck) in one hand and turn the collar sleeve counterclockwise with your other hand. This action will open the jaws of the chuck. Turn until the opening of the chuck is large enough to insert the

bit. Insert the bit and tighten the chuck, turning clockwise—make sure it's good and tight. When tightening (closing) or loosening (opening) the chuck, clockwise or counterclockwise changes with orientation—my indications are from a perspective where I'm looking at the drill with the chuck facing me.

- **To drive a screw:** Rotate the adjustable clutch ring (it will be numbered) to a midrange number (this will vary depending on your drill—read the instructions). Make sure your forward/reverse switch is in the forward mode (which means the bit will turn clockwise—again, read the instructions to familiarize yourself with where this switch is). With the driver bit loaded in the chuck, place the screw on the tip of your bit. Now put the tip of the screw on the surface you will drive through. Gently squeeze the trigger, applying steady but light pressure on the drill until the screw's threads catch the material—you may need to use short trigger bursts at first to make this happen. Once the threads catch, continue squeezing the trigger, maintaining pressure on the drill until the screw is sunk to the desired depth.

FYI, torque, or turning power, will increase as you rotate your clutch from lower to higher numbers. A clutch is designed to disengage the drive shaft (turning mechanism) when it reaches a preset resistance (the clutch number you set it to). This means you'll hear the motor running, but the bit won't be spinning (you'll also hear a clicking sound). For example, when driving a small screw, you would use a low clutch setting. At this low setting, if you mistakenly hold the trigger down once the screw is already driven, the resistance will "tell" the clutch to disengage, stopping the bit from spinning, and preventing you from stripping your screw head or driving the screw too deeply. The higher numbers are for longer and harder surfaces. The "drill" position, usually indicated after the highest clutch number in a drill by symbol, is used when you want full drilling and driving power with no clutch.

- **To drive a drill bit:** Rotate the clutch ring to the "drill" setting (this will vary depending on your drill—read the instructions). With the drill bit loaded, hold the drill and place the bit on the desired drilling spot. Apply gentle pressure and begin squeezing the trigger—the bit will start to bore through the material. Continue squeezing the trigger and maintain steady pressure until the bit is sunk to the desired depth.

Drilling Tips

- Always maintain control of the drill by holding it firmly in your hands.
- Beware of letting loose clothing, hair, jewelry, etc., dangle near the rotating bit.
- Bits or screws will get hot if spinning in material for more than a few seconds — touching them could burn you.
- Wear safety glasses.
- Make a pilot hole (a starter hole) with a small drill bit before driving the actual screw.
- When drilling through metal, use graduating-size drill bits to make holes until you reach the desired hole size.
- If the screw snags in the material, don't forget that there's a "reverse" switch to easily back it out.
- For ease of sinking longer screws, first scrape wax (from a candle) on the threads, then drive it in.

Between a best friend and a power drill a girl can do just about anything!

Power drill

PLASTER WALL REPAIR

Unlike drywall, plaster walls will not incur the same types of holes as drywall because they are not hollow. Behind the plaster is lath (thin strips of wood) to which plaster is applied through a painstaking and time-consuming multistep trowel process (part of the reason why they're not being used anymore). Cracks and small holes, however, are typical in plaster walls. A "hole" in plaster is not really a hole but rather an area where the plaster has broken away from the lath, exposing it. If you do manage to get a large "hole" (over several inches in diameter) or a hole exposing damaged lath, I suggest calling a friend or pro who has experience repairing plaster walls.

Repairing Cracks and Holes in Plaster Walls

TOOLS
- Newspaper
- 4-inch putty knife
- Rag
- Joint compound
- Dust mask
- Medium-grit sanding block
- Spray elastic crack sealant
- Primer and paint

1. Place newspaper on the floor under the crack or hole.
2. With the corner tip of the putty blade, clean out any loose plaster. Wipe it down with a rag to make sure that it's all cleaned out.
3. Load the putty knife with joint compound. At a forty-five-degree angle to the wall, press the compound into the hole while passing the blade diagonally (left to right) along the surface of the hole and wall. Be sure that the entire crack or hole is filled, so reload your knife and go over it if necessary.
4. Allow the patch to dry for several hours. Once it's dry, check to see if the joint compound has shrunk, leaving indentations. If this is the case, the patch will need another layer of compound. Repeat steps 3–5, only this time pass the blade diagonally from right to left

(this will fill in misses from the opposite direction — it works great).

5. Once it's all white and powdery, you can sand it, being sure to smooth the edges where the patch meets the wall surface. Wear a dust mask when sanding. Wipe the patch to clean off the dust.

6. Paint the repair with a primer or your matching flat wall color. If your wall has a shine to its paint finish, like eggshell or semigloss, you must give it a coat of primer or flat paint first — paint that has a shine to its finish will "flash" directly over a patch, which means it will leave a visible difference in finish compared to the rest of the wall.

Skim Coating

"Skim coating" sounds like I'm advocating the bone-strengthening benefits of eating a diet rich in low-fat dairy products, doesn't it? But while I am a big fan of yogurt and cottage cheese, in this case skim coating refers to a wall-finishing process in which a thin layer of joint compound (aka mud or plaster) is applied over the surface of a wall to create an extremely smooth and hard coating.

You would typically skim-coat a wall that has seen better days — with interspersed areas of chipping paint, dents, and cracks. One that's not in bad enough condition to take down entirely, but whose surface definitely needs a face lift.

I have to admit I hesitated to write about this fix. "Hey, make an old wall look like new — what's the problem with that?" There *is* no problem — if you're a seasoned plasterer who can wield a trowel like my grandmother did a spatula. There's an art to plastering that isn't perfected in one project. So here's my advice and my reason for including skim coating in the book:

- Keep in mind that most worthwhile things aren't easily attained or accomplished.
- Start small — don't try to take on an entire room on your first try.
- Practice on a wall in the garage or a large scrap of drywall.
- Remember that you're a strong woman and you can do anything you put your mind to.

The following skim-coating method comes directly from Cousin Sal. I personally find this the easiest and best way to get it done right.

TOOLS
- Drop cloth
- 6-inch putty knife
- Ladder
- 12-inch trowel
- Joint compound
- Dust mask
- Safety glasses
- Medium-grit sanding block
- Rag
- Oil-based primer
- Paint of your choice

1. Lay the drop cloth along the floor of the wall you'll be working on.
2. With the putty knife, scrape the wall surface, removing any loose paint, plaster, and wallboard.
3. Position your ladder under one corner of the wall—you'll be starting from one corner and working your way to the other. Load the trowel with a big scoop of joint compound and climb up the ladder.
4. Feeding from the trowel, load your putty knife with a small fist-size amount of joint compound. You will be applying the compound in three-foot-wide strips running vertically down your walls. Holding the knife at approximately a forty-five-degree angle to the wall, begin pressing and spreading the joint compound down the wall. Work a three-foot-wide space, smearing the compound in vertical passes. Spread this layer as smooth and thin as possible. When you get down to an uncomfortable position on the ladder, step off the ladder and continue the same process to the bottom of the wall.
5. With one vertical strip complete, move your ladder over 3 feet and begin your second strip, following the same process. Continue these steps until the entire wall surface is covered. Keep in mind

that less is more, so don't put on a heavy coat. Concentrate on smooth and thin—you know, the way we want our thighs to look!

6. Let it dry for several hours.

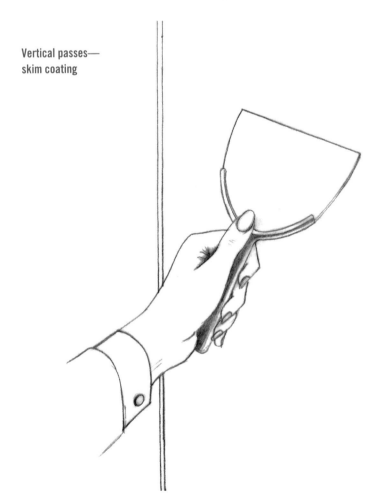

Vertical passes—skim coating

7. Put on the dust mask and safety glasses and, with the sanding block, knock down any obviously raised edges (this is a light sanding, so don't spend too much time with it).

8. Now you're ready for the second coat. (Oh, did I forget to mention there'd be a second coat? Sorry.) You will repeat steps 3–6, only this time, instead of spreading the compound vertically, you'll do it horizontally. Changing directions will give you an opportunity to better fill in crevices. Be sure to smooth out and "feather" any ridges, especially where the strips meet. Your goal is to create one even surface.

9. This second coat will dry quickly. When it's all white and powdery, put on your dust mask and safety glasses and sand down the entire wall. There will be a lot of dust, so be prepared. Make sure you sand as evenly as possible, so don't get carried away in one spot.

10. When the sanding is completed, wipe off any dust with a soft rag.

11. Prime the wall with an oil-based primer before painting your color. I specify oil-based because, although it's not as easy to work

with as latex, it seals the skim coat better than latex does (oil based paints don't clean up with water, so work neatly). Once the wall is primed, it is now ready for any paint you fancy.

Repairing Nail Pops

Nail pops are unsightly bumps created by nails in the studs behind your walls that are visible through your wall or ceiling. Sometimes the nail will pop so far that it will actually cause the drywall to flake off, revealing the head of the nail. Why does this happen? Two reasons. There could have been an error during the installation—the installer may not have pressed the wallboard firmly enough against the lumber when fastening. That gap leaves room for the nail to pop. The other reason for nail pops is lumber shrinkage. As the lumber dries and moves away from the drywall, the nail may not move along with it—and pop goes the weasel. This project will show you how to remove the popped nail and refasten the drywall to the wall stud correctly so that it won't happen again.

TOOLS
- Newspaper
- Putty knife
- Power drill/driver
- Several 1-inch drywall screws
- Hammer
- Joint compound
- Medium-grit sanding block
- Rag
- Primer and paint

1. Place newspaper on the floor under the hole to protect your floor from splattering joint compound and plaster particles.
2. With your putty knife, scrape off the raised drywall caused by the pop—being sure to clear away any loose debris.
3. Set a screw about a 1½ inches above or below the pop, pressing against the drywall and being sure to hit the stud. (This will refasten that section. No point in trying to reset the popped fastener.)

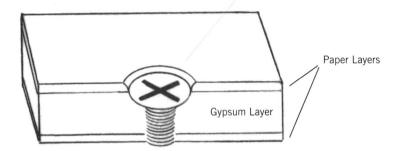

Dimple,
but don't break through
the paper layer

Paper Layers

Gypsum Layer

Sink the screw into the wall far enough to dimple the drywall, but not far enough to tear the paper of the drywall.

4. Remove the old nail with the claw of your hammer or, if it's a screw, unscrew it with the power drill.

5. To patch, load the putty knife with a walnut-size amount of joint compound. Holding the knife at approximately a forty-five-degree angle to the wall, press the compound into the hole while passing the blade diagonally (left to right) along the surface of the hole and wall. Be sure that the entire hole is filled, so go over it if you must. It is normal for excess plaster to spread beyond the edges of the hole.

6. Allow the patch to dry for several hours. Once it's dry, check to see if the joint compound has shrunk, leaving indentations. If this is the case, the patch will need another layer of compound. Repeat steps 3–5, only this time pass the blade diagonally from right to left (this will fill in misses from the opposite direction — it works great). Allow it to dry.

7. Once the compound is all white and powdery, you can sand it, being sure to smooth the edges where the patch meets the wall surface. Wipe the patch with a rag to clean off the dust.

8. Paint the repair with a primer or your matching flat wall color. If your wall has a shine to its paint finish, like eggshell or semigloss,

you must give it a coat of primer or flat paint first. Paint that has a shine to its finish will "flash" directly over a patch, which means it will leave a visible difference in finish compared to the rest of the wall, unless you prime it.

Chix Tip: How I Get Nailed— I'm Talkin' Manicures

Speaking of nails, let's talk about manicures. People always ask me how I keep my nails looking so great with the type of work I do. I think sometimes men are suspicious of whether I really do the work on my show myself. Yeah, guys, I'm just a girl they found who looks cute in a tool belt. The calluses on my palms and black-and-blue spots on my arms are put there by my makeup artist. Oh, and she sprays the sweat onto my brow, too.

When women ask me, though, they just want to know my secrets. Well, ladies, here they are:

- Good genes—my grandmother had nails you could use to mine granite.
- Drink plenty of water and take vitamins.
- Go for manicures regularly.

I never leave my nails unpolished. Like raw wood, unprotected nails split and crack. Oddly, the more I work with my hands, the stronger my nails get! I have a theory about this. Because blood nourishes your nails from the nail bed, the more circulation in your hands, the stronger your nails become. I thought this was just another one of my "I betcha" ideas until I shared it with Holly, our camerawoman on *Toolbelt Diva*. She raises horses and explained to me that when horses are inactive, their hooves get all weak and soft. Guess I nailed that theory!

Wearing a mask

GETTING RID OF WALL STAINS

Before I can tell you how to get rid of a wall stain, you have to determine how it got there in the first place. Painting over them doesn't work—stains almost always burn through the paint and become visible again. Below are techniques for removing many common wall stains I've seen and conquered.

Removing Mold and Mildew

These stains may appear as black spots or fuzzy patches. Whatever they look like, they're ugly, potentially dangerous, and have got to go!

Wear safety glasses, gloves, and a respirator (with a filter specific for mold) to scrub down the walls with a solution of 1 part bleach and 4 parts water or a mold-and-mildew cleaner (available in any hardware store). Rinse the walls. Once they're dry, prime them with a good-quality primer.

Something important to think about: Mold and mildew can cause health problems. So whatever is causing the mold to grow—excessive dampness, poor ventilation—must be corrected!

Removing Water Stains

Ugly water ring stains have got to go. But before treating the stain, you need to treat the leak! Once your leak is corrected, and you're sure the drywall is sound (poke at it to make sure there's no other damage besides stains), prime with an alcohol-based primer and then paint over the stain. My personal experience is that alcohol-based primers cover water stains best. The only problem is they stink to high heaven, so wear a mask or respirator (if the warning label recommends it) and work in a ventilated area!

Removing Organic-Matter Stains (Food, Grease, Etc.)

Scrub with a detergent. If your walls are painted with a flat finish, it's highly likely that this process will actually remove the paint. Rinse the walls. Once they're dry, you can prime and paint.

Removing Smoke Damage

Wash the walls with an all-purpose cleaner. Scrub away the black residue as much as possible without damaging the wall surface. Rinse the walls. Once they're dry, prime and paint.

Removing Pen and Marker Stains

Listen to me: *Never use a pen or marker on your walls,* not even if you're planning on painting them and are marking measurements. *Only use pencil.* Pen and marker burn through primers the way I burn through my paycheck at a shoe sale. They're almost impossible to get rid of. I remember my cousin Sal and I were working in a house where the owner's young son went Picasso with a red pen all over his bedroom walls. We tried everything. We scrubbed. We primed. Reprimed. Tried new primers that claimed to be the best on the market. We painted. Repainted. That red pen always burned through. It was getting scary—like we were afraid we'd come in the next day and it would spell out "redrum." Finally the only alternative was to give the homeowner two choices: (a) take the walls down and put up new or (b) go with a fire-engine theme and paint them red. She went with the red. Sometimes when life gives you lemons, make lemonade.

HANGING WALL OBJECTS

I recently moved into a new apartment. I thought unpacking was going to be a pain, but the thing that proved the most time-consuming? Hanging things. Mirrors, shelves, pictures, curtain rods, candle sconces, artwork, stemware rack—if I didn't have the right materials and know-how to get these jobs done, I'm sure I'd have wanted to hang myself!

Whether your walls are drywall or plaster (see "Drywall and Plaster Anatomies and Remedies, page 126)" putting a naked screw in them to hang something just doesn't work. The drywall will be hollow (unless you hit a stud), and the screw will just wobble around. The plaster will be too brittle and will simply crumble if you try to sink a screw. Hence the birth of these fabulous little inventions called wall anchors and toggle bolts. Basically, they provide a mounting system for the screw to do its job. They come in various styles and are made of various materials, but they all have the same job: to hold that screw in place to support whatever it is you're hanging.

Plastic Wall Anchors

Plastic anchors are very common. They come in different sizes that use different-size screws (screws and anchors are often sold together in a set). You should follow any weight limitations on their packaging. For general purposes, like hanging a towel rack or a small shelf, they work great.

TOOLS
- Pencil
- Nail punch
- Hammer
- Drill bit and drill (if you're going through plaster)
- Plastic anchor and appropriate screws
- Phillips screwdriver

1. With your object in place against the wall, use a pencil to mark the spot where you'll need to sink the screw.
2. Remove the object. With the nail punch and hammer, tap a small hole into the wall where you marked it. If you're going through plaster, drill a starter hole (aka pilot hole) with a drill bit slightly smaller than the size of your anchor.
3. Place the anchor over the hole and tap it into the wall with the hammer until it becomes flush with the wall.
4. Put your object in place, lining up the hole of the object with the hole of the anchor, and drive the screw in with the screwdriver.

Chix Tip: Ook

Let me talk about a product I just adore—OOK Art & Picture Hanging Hardware. This product is so well designed I want to kiss the genius who developed it! No studs, no anchors, no fuss, no muss—all you have to do is tap the tiny blue steel pins through the hanging bracket and into the wall and you can hang almost anything. I hung two seventy-five-pound mirrors for my aunt Rose-Marie on the wall behind her couch that are held up by these hooks—and have been for five years now. They come in sizes that can hold from five to a hundred pounds. And all that's left when you remove the hanger are minuscule pinholes. You gotta love that! So when it comes to hanging mirrors, frames, plates, and pictures, OOK is the must-have.

Self-Drilling Plastic Anchors

These are a newer version of plastic anchors, except with these the anchor screws in, as opposed to being hammered in.

Self-drilling plastic anchor

TOOLS
- Pencil
- Nail punch
- Hammer
- Drill bit and drill (if you're going through plaster)
- Self-drilling plastic anchor and appropriate screws
- Phillips screwdriver

1. With your object in place against the wall, use a pencil to mark the spot where you'll need to sink the screw.
2. Remove the object. With the nail punch and hammer, tap a small hole into the wall where you marked it. If you're going through plaster, drill a starter hole (aka pilot hole) with a drill bit slightly smaller than the size of your anchor.
3. Place the anchor over the hole and screw it in with a screwdriver.
4. Put your object in place, lining up the hole of the object with the hole of the anchor, and drive the screw in with the screwdriver.

Chix Tip:
Leveling Hanging Objects

Installing an object that requires one screw is easy. But what happens when you need two screws—one on either end—like on a towel rack? That's when the level needs to come out.

1. Place your object on the wall and mark with a pencil where one hole will go.
2. Follow the steps listed under the appropriate project heading for installing the proper fastener.
3. Measure the distance between the two holes on the object. Take that measurement and mark with a pencil that distance from the first hole you made, making a long straight line.
4. Place your level against the wall, lining up one end of it with the first hole, and raise and lower the other end over the pencil mark you made until the bubble centers, reading level. Mark that point with a horizontal line over the vertical one and voilà! X marks the spot—that's where the second hole goes!

Line crossing for point marking

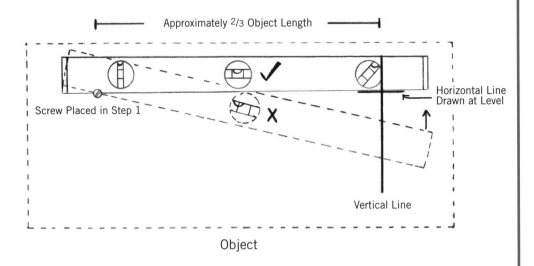

Molly Bolts (or Sleeved Anchors)

Molly bolts are great for heavier objects like shelves or a larger mirror. A standard-type molly is for plaster walls, and a drive-type is for drywall.

Molly bolt

TOOLS
- Pencil
- Drill bit and drill (if you're going through plaster)
- Hammer
- Molly bolt (or sleeved anchor)
- Phillips screwdriver

1. With your object in place against the wall, use a pencil to mark the spot where you'll need to sink the screw.
2. Remove the object. If you're going through plaster, drill a pilot hole where the screw will go with a drill bit slightly smaller than the size of your anchor. The drive-type molly for wallboard just hammers in, no pilot hole needed.
3. Using a hammer, drive the anchor *with the screw a quarter of the way inserted in the anchor itself.* Once the molly is flush to the wall, drive the screw clockwise, pressing firmly, until you feel the sleeve lock against the back of the wall.
4. Now remove the screw, using a screwdriver and turning counter-clockwise.
5. Put your object in place, lining up the hole of the object with the hole of the anchor, and drive the screw in with the screwdriver.

Toggle Bolts

Toggle bolts are excellent for heavy objects but a little trickier to install. The "wings" of this bolt open as you screw it in place and lock up against the back of the wall.

One major consideration with this type of bolt is you must drive a large pilot hole through the wall first that will allow the closed wings to pass through it. Keep in mind that whatever you hang using a toggle bolt must be large enough to cover this hole.

Toggle bolt

TOOLS
- Pencil
- Nail punch
- Hammer
- Drill bit and drill (if you're going through plaster)
- Toggle bolt (long enough to fit through the object you're hanging, the length of the wings, plus 1 inch for thickness of your wall)
- Phillips screwdriver

1. With your object in place against the wall, use a pencil to mark the spot where you'll need to sink the bolt.
2. Remove the object. Using a nail punch and hammer, tap a hole into the wall large enough to fit the toggle. If you're going through plaster, drill a starter hole (aka pilot hole) with a drill bit that will make a hole large enough to allow the toggle to pass through it.
3. Put your object in place, lining up the hole of the object with the hole for the toggle. Slide the bolt through your object, then screw the wings onto the back of the bolt (the opened wings should face the head of the bolt). Now pinch the wings closed and slide the bolt, wings attached, through the hole you made in the wall. Once the wings pass through the wall, they will spring open.
4. To secure your object in place, you will have to pull back on it while screwing the bolt until the wings press against and create resistance with the back of the wall—if not, the screw will just spin and spin.
5. Continue tightening with your screwdriver until the object is snug against the wall.

Finding a Stud

It's actually fabulous when you hit a stud when sinking a screw in the wall. No anchors, toggle bolts, pilot holes—just screw right in, but to get it to sink properly, you need a coarse-threaded drywall screw that's at least $1\frac{1}{4}$ inch long. Securing a fastener directly into a stud is the most secure way to mount anything. But how do you find one?

I used to think that finding a stud involved responding to personal ads, carousing in bars, and suffering through blind dates. But in construction a stud quest has nothing to do with meeting men. In fact, there are dozens of studs all around you right now!

If you want to make sure something is really *well hung* (you see why I love construction?!), you have to start by finding a stud—an upright in the framing of a building to which sheathing, paneling, wallboard, or lath is fastened. Below are a couple of cool ways to find them. (Word to the wise: I wouldn't recommend either method when trying to find a stud to take you out to dinner!)

Old-School Stud Finding: This method simply involves knocking on the wall and listening. Move horizontally across the wall, tapping every few inches. At some point the knock will sound more like a thud than a hollow echo. Most likely the thud is the stud. Generally, studs are 16 inches apart, which means when you find one, you can measure 16 inches to the right or left of it to find the next stud. Another trick is knocking to the left or right of an electrical outlet. Outlet boxes are often screwed right onto a stud, so that can be a good starting point.

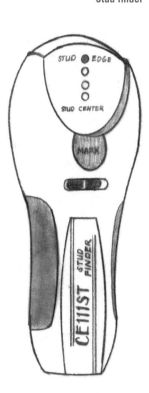

Stud finder

High-Tech Method of Stud Finding: A stud finder senses the density, or thickness, of what its plate is touching. When it goes over wallboard, which is thinner than a stud, it senses low density. When there is a stud behind the wallboard, the stud finder can tell that it's hit a higher-density area. Most stud finders emit a blinking light to let you know they're working. Slowly glide the finder across your wall until the light becomes steady or it beeps (depending on the particular model), indicating that it senses the stud. Stud finders range widely in price and function. There are even some sensors that indicate whether you've found wood, pipes, or live wiring!

Whichever method you use, always test your finding

first with a small nail. If the nail hammers through very easily and wobbles around, you're not in the stud. When you hit wood, the nail will let you know it!

WALLPAPER REPAIRS

When wallpaper is well hung it can make a room look fabulous (not to mention what it can do for a guy in a pair of tight jeans!). But when edges curl or scratches become obvious it can make an entire room look tired and raggedy. Happily, freshening up wallpaper is a fast and fret-free fix!

Removing Blisters

A blister or bubble in wallpaper is almost always due to an air gap. To get rid of it, you need to open the gap up and let the air pass. Gas-X won't work for this, though—you'll use another type of X.

TOOLS
- Single-edge razor blade
- Heavy-duty wallpaper-border adhesive
- Glue-injecting syringe
- Clean, damp, soft rag

Injecting adhesive

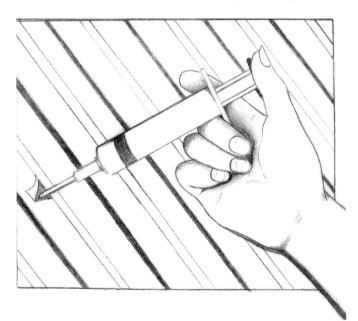

1. With a new, sharp razor blade, cut an X in the center of the blister.
2. Gently peel back the X, being sure not to tear the paper.
3. Inject some adhesive around the opening, and with the tip of the syringe, under the paper.
4. Press the X closed and carefully smooth down the repaired area, first with your fingers, then with a damp rag.

Fixing Curled Edges

TOOLS
- Clean, damp, soft rag
- Old paintbrush
- Heavy-duty wallpaper-border adhesive
- Wallpaper roller

1. Peel back the curling paper until it reaches the point where it's still stuck on the wall. Do not crease it!
2. Use a rag to wipe away any dried glue that's flaking off.
3. With an old paintbrush, apply the adhesive to the wall.
4. Press the paper over the adhesive and smooth it down with your hand, being sure to smooth in the direction of the seam so that air will escape as you're pressing—you don't want to leave any air gaps.
5. With the wallpaper roller, roll over the repair, then down the seam.
6. Wipe off the surface with a damp rag.

Wallpaper patch

Repairing Scratches and Other Damage

TOOLS
- Scrap of matching wallpaper
- Old paintbrush
- Heavy-duty wallpaper-border adhesive
- Single-edge razor blade
- Clean, damp, soft rag
- Wallpaper roller

1. Find a piece of scrap that matches the pattern on your paper. This repair piece must be at least 1 inch larger than the damaged area all around.
2. With an old paintbrush, apply adhesive to the back of the repair piece and let it sit until it gets tacky.
3. Align the repair piece over the damaged area

and press it in place, being sure to match the pattern and leaving about an inch extra around the edges of the damaged spot.

4. With a new sharp razor blade, cut out the damaged section, piercing through both the patch and the old paper. Don't make perfectly straight lines—patches look better when the seams are random.

5. Carefully peel away first the repair piece, then the damaged portion, then the excess.

6. With a rag, wipe clean the now-opened wall surface, then brush on the adhesive.

7. Align the repair piece over the hole and smooth down the patch with your hands. Make sure to let any air escape out the seams.

8. With the wallpaper roller, roll over the repair, then down the seams.

9. Wipe off the surface with a damp rag.

FLOOR TILES

Is it possible for a room to look beautiful if it has picture-perfect walls but a floor that looks like circus animals just trampled through it? I don't think so. That's like trying to look fetching in a cocktail dress with Birkenstocks and socks. Fabulous flooring starts here with floor tile at the top of the list.

Replacing a Ceramic Tile

Whether it's a damaged ceramic tile in your hallway or a loose one in your shower stall, the repair is the same. If you don't have spare tiles, bring the broken tile piece with you to a home center or hardware store to find an exact or similar replacement. Know that this repair will take two days to complete because of drying times.

FYI, this repair works on a tiled wall as well. Keep in mind when you're repairing a tile on a vertical surface such as a bathroom or shower wall to protect the surrounding area—tub, floor, whatever—with a drop cloth.

TOOLS

- Grout saw
- Stiff metal putty knife
- Masonry chisel
- Hammer
- Safety glasses
- Notched trowel
- Replacement tile
- Mastic (tile adhesive)
- Rubber mallet or hammer
- Plastic tile spacers or cardboard
- Utility knife
- Rubber float
- Matching grout
- Bucket
- Waterproof gloves
- Large sponge
- Soft cloth
- Grout sealer

1. With a grout saw, remove the grout surrounding the tile you want to replace. This will make a clean joint for regrouting, give you a space to angle your tool to pry out the old tile, and help you to avoid damaging adjacent ones.

2. If the tile is loose, pry it off with a small putty knife. If the tile's damaged but still stuck on there, you'll need to break it out in small pieces using a chisel and hammer—wear safety glasses. Be careful not to go overboard with the chiseling, because you don't want to damage the submaterial.

3. Once the tile is out, clean the surface of remaining mastic, tile bits, and grout using a putty knife.

4. With a notched trowel, back-butter (love that expression) the new tile—spreading mastic on the back of the tile—about $\frac{1}{4}$ to $\frac{1}{2}$ inch thick (try to match the depth of the existing tile).

5. Place the "buttered" tile into the space and press it down—you can use a rubber mallet or hammer handle to help tap it in place. Your

goal is to match the depth of the existing tile, so you may need to add or remove some adhesive. Also, you must center the tile so the joint is evenly spaced all the way around. You may need to use plastic tile spacers or folded pieces of cardboard to maintain the space while it dries.

6. With a putty or utility knife, clean out any mastic that may have oozed into the joint. Wipe the face of the tile clean as well. Now let it dry for twenty-four hours.

7. Once the mastic has dried, you can apply the grout. With a rubber float (looks like a rubber-sided trowel), press and spread the grout into the joints. Once they're filled, slide the float with the edge of the float raised at an angle to remove excess grout.

Grouting tile with float

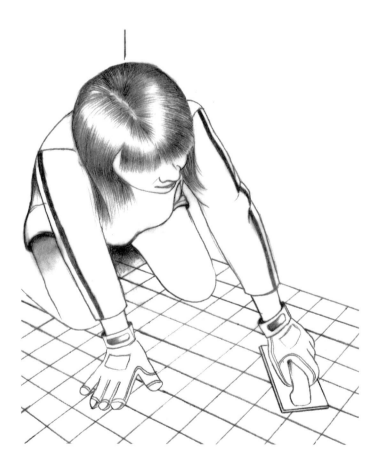

8. Fill a bucket halfway with clean water. With a large, clean, and fully damp sponge, wipe down the tile, gently smoothing over the grout lines—being careful not to pull the grout out. Keep rinsing the sponge so you work with it as clean as possible.

9. After about a half hour, you'll see a powdery haze form over the tiles—wipe it down with a soft cloth, polishing until shiny.

10. It is recommended that a grout sealer be applied at least two days later to protect the grout from water damage and staining and chipping.

Replacing a Vinyl Tile

It's easy to pick up and replace damaged vinyl tiles—if you know all the tricks!

TOOLS
- Gloves
- Stiff metal putty knife
- Matching replacement tile
- Vinyl floor adhesive
- Notched trowel
- Rag
- Waxed paper
- A few heavy books

1. Wearing gloves, work the tip of a putty knife into the most visible joint of the tile you need to replace. Continue wedging and scraping until the entire tile is lifted.

2. With the putty knife, scrape away any adhesive or tile bits left on the subfloor.

Chix Safety Tip for Asbestos

If you live in an older home (1970s and earlier), it is possible that your tiles are made of asbestos, especially if they are 9 by 9 inches—a distinctive asbestos tile size. Now, just because asbestos tiles are in your home, that doesn't automatically mean they pose a risk to your health. Asbestos is dangerous only when the particles become airborne—like when they're being broken out for removal! Before starting any tile replacement, you should have them tested by an EPA-approved testing lab. You can also purchase an asbestos home test kit.

Chix Safety Tip for Tile

Broken tile pieces are like slivers of glass. You must wear protective hand and eye gear when cutting or handling cut pieces of tile.

3. If what you're replacing is a peel-and-stick tile, just peel and stick! Oh, and press, too. Or, if adhesive is required, apply glue to the space with a notched trowel, let it get tacky, then position and drop in the tile, pressing it in place.

4. Use a rag to wipe the joints of any adhesive that may have oozed out.

5. Place a piece of waxed paper over the patch and weight it down overnight with some heavy books.

6. Let the tile dry for twenty-four hours before walking on it.

Patching Vinyl Flooring

You know when you want to clean behind your refrigerator 'cause you're feeling really ambitious and environmentally conscious and you're inspired to harvest all the dust fields and mold cultures that have been growing under there? And when you're pulling out that big ol' fridge, feeling pretty damn good about yourself, it's just then that you gouge a huge scratch right through the vinyl floor!

Now you're telling yourself, "Great! That's what I get for trying to do the right thing. I'd have been better off just wiping down the damn door with some Windex, calling it a day, and spending the rest of the afternoon napping on the couch!"

But don't panic. After you're done cursing and kicking the refrigerator, you can follow these simple steps to fix that floor.

TOOLS
- Scrap of matching flooring
- Duct tape
- Straightedge (i.e., framing square or metal level)
- Utility knife
- Putty knife

Chix Tricks: Remove Vinyl Flooring with a Little Heat

If you are trying to remove a damaged vinyl tile (or sheet flooring) and it just keeps breaking off in annoying little bits, there's a trick to help you pry it off with ease. With a handheld plumber's blowtorch or electric heat gun, you can heat up the tile, which will loosen the adhesive, making it easy to pry up the tile. Just sweep the gun or blowtorch (follow igniting directions) back and forth over the tile, never stopping in one place (which would cause the tile to burn, as opposed to heat up). Once the tile is hot and the glue is gooey, use the scraper to peel it up.

- Vinyl floor adhesive
- Notched trowel
- Waxed paper
- A few heavy books
- Liquid seam sealer

1. Take a piece of scrap flooring, place it over the scratch, and align it so that it encompasses one entire flooring pattern. Make sure that the scrap piece is large enough to cover one whole pattern plus a couple of inches extra all the way around.
2. With the scrap piece properly lined up, tape it to the floor with duct tape.
3. Using a straightedge and a sharp utility knife, cut out the full pattern, slicing through both the scrap and the existing tile. It will take a few passes.
4. Remove the tape and the scrap piece (which is now cut to the identical patch size). Peel up the old damaged piece with a putty knife and scrape away any adhesive left on the subfloor.
5. Take the replacement patch and dry-fit it—make slight adjustments if necessary with the utility knife and bevel the undersides of the edges slightly to help it join and lay in seamlessly.
6. Apply adhesive to the space with a notched trowel, let it get tacky, and then position and drop in the patch, pressing it in place.
7. Wipe the joints of any adhesive that may have oozed out.
8. Place a piece of waxed paper over the patch and weight it down overnight with some heavy books.
9. The following day apply a liquid seam sealer, following the product directions.

HOW TO HANDLE HARDWOOD FLOORS

Squeaky Floors

Squeaky floors are annoying and potentially dangerous. Often a squeak means that a floorboard is coming up, and this could be a tripping hazard that you will inevitably discover late one night with your big toe.

Squeaks that appear suddenly and quickly become much worse should not be ignored, since they may be signs of trouble. For example, a new squeak may indicate a leak under the flooring. Best to check it out.

Once you've identified the problem, there are a couple of ways to proceed.

Fixing Buckled Floorboards

If it is obvious that the floorboards have buckled up and there is no evidence of active water damage or floor joists (the beams floors are nailed to) sagging, the easiest fix is just to nail the floorboards back down from the top.

TOOLS
- 10d or 12d finishing nails
- Hammer
- Nail set
- $1\frac{1}{4}$-inch wood screw
- 1-inch putty knife
- Wood patch
- Sharpie or carpenter's crayon
- Drill

1. Locate the buckle.
2. Use a fairly large finishing nail, 10d or 12d. Hammer through the floorboard all the way into the joist. Do not nail into the seam where two floorboards meet. Be careful not to mar the floor with the head of the hammer. To countersink the nail, put the nail set over the nail and hammer until the nail sits slightly deeper than the surface of the wood (creating a slight dimple in the wood). Countersinking the nail creates a small indention (dimple) for a filler (in this case, wood patch) to cover the nail head.
3. With a putty knife, use a wood patch to cover the nail hole, follow the product directions.

If you have access to the underside of the floor through an unfinished basement or a crawl space, a variation on this fix is to screw from below, going through the subfloor and into the finished floor at the trouble spot.

1. Enlist a friend and have her walk around the room and locate the squeaks while you have a look underneath. Often there will be a space between the floor joist and the subfloor at the trouble spot, and you may see a little bounce in the wood. Mark all the problems with a Sharpie or a carpenter's crayon.

2. Have your friend stand on the spot while you drive the screw to hold the boards down. Make sure that you use a screw long enough to do the job but short enough so that it doesn't come through the face—a $1\frac{1}{4}$-inch screw should do the trick. With a drill, screw into the subfloor and up into, but not through, the finished floor.

Fixing a Sagging Floor Joist

Sometimes the floorboards are sound but the floor joist has sagged, creating a gap. This may be normal, especially if the house is older and the gap is small and isolated. A large gap or a whole area like this can be a sign of a more serious foundation problem and should be checked out by a professional. Needless to say, if there is any evidence of wood damage, you should have a contractor address the problem right away. Mold, rot, and insect damage left unchecked can continue to spread and wind up costing you a fortune!

For minor joist sagging, the following fixes are applicable only if you have access to the underside of the floor through an unfinished basement or a crawl space—sorry, there's just no other way to get to the joist.

Chix Tip: Know Your Nail Lingo

Dor "penny," as nails are also referred to, is the unit of measurement for nail sizes. These terms originate from "pence," or penny, which originally came from the Roman coin *denarius*, hence the "d." The larger the "d," the larger the nail. Nails range from 2d, which measure 1 inch long, to 40d, which measure 5 inches long.

TOOLS
- Wood shims
- Hammer
- Several 2-inch wood screws
- Length of 2x4 (cut to 1 foot longer than the length of trouble spot on either side)
- Construction adhesive
- Drill

1. Examine the area to determine where there is sagging in the joist and gaps between the joist and the subfloor.
2. Slide shims into these gaps and hammer them until they're snug.

AN ALTERNATE JOIST FIX

1. Run a bead of construction adhesive along the top of the 2x4 (on the 2-inch edge).
2. Put the board up, alongside the joist, with the adhesive side pressed into the subfloor, and use the drill to screw this "splint" into the joist. Drive a screw every 4 inches.

Maintaining Finish

If it has been a number of years since your floors were finished, the surface may not be very well protected. Modern polyurethane is extremely tough, but even it can wear through over time, particularly in high-traffic areas. Older floors may have been finished with shellac or even wax. Neither of these will resist much wear, and older floors are often quite dark from years without protection. Short of a full-scale refinishing, there is not much you can do when wood has become dark or damaged. Your best bet may be to try one of the mop-on floor-refinishing products on the market. Check with your paint store to see what brand it carries.

The best way to maintain the appearance of your wood floors is to protect them from damage in the first place. Keep these tips in mind for all of your hardwood floors:

- **Clean up spills right away.** Liquids can damage your floor, so take care to mop and dry spill areas immediately.

- **Mop and dust floors regularly.** All you have to do to maintain your poly finish is regular sweeping or vacuuming and mopping with a product like Murphy's Oil Soap or a solution of white vinegar and warm water. Don't use harsh detergents as over time they may dull a finish.

- **Clean up after your pets.** Animals that spend a lot of time outdoors track a tremendous amount of sand into your house, which is very abrasive to your floor. Also, a pet's nails are tough on the finish, so keep Fang's claws clipped.

- **Cover chair and table legs with glides.** A common problem with wood floors is that they are easily scratched by furniture. Make sure that you have felt or plastic glides on your chair legs, and never drag furniture across a wood floor.

- **Use rugs in high-traffic areas.** Protect your floors from constant foot traffic with durable area rugs.

- **Don't wax your floors.** Just because your mother waxed her wood floors doesn't mean you should. Floors that are finished with polyurethane, including virtually all floors installed within the last thirty years, do not require waxing. In fact, since wax has a tendency to yellow, it will make your floor look worse over time. Since the poly finish blocks the wax from being absorbed into the wood grain, wax simply accumulates on the surface as a goopy yellow buildup.

- **Camouflage scratches with tinted wax or furniture polish.** Rub in a little of either one with a cotton cloth and poof—scratches are almost gone. If you're not sure of the color to use, start with a lighter shade. It's easy to add color but tough to get rid of it. If your floor is light to begin with, using a touch-up color that is too dark might make the patch more visible than the scratch!

Chix Chat:
Please Remove Your Shoes

Once I was living in a small studio apartment in L.A. When I say small, I mean *small*. This apartment made a shoe box seem palatial—especially ironic since I had more shoe boxes than living space and was forced to convert a stack of them into an end table.

Three weeks after I moved into this apart*mini*, I invited over some crew members to discuss future show projects. We sit down, elbow to elbow, and right away I start to smell the foulest odor words can describe. It was a cross between dirty diapers and Bourbon Street on Sunday morning. What the hell could be stinking like that? One by one I see my coworkers' noses twitching. I'm thinking, *Could I have forgotten to take out the garbage for about a month?* No. Then it hit me.

"Hey, guys, could you check your shoes?" Sure enough, Hartman's shoe was absolutely slathered in dog poop, and he had tracked it all over my tiny apartment (which took all of about three steps). So basically the entire carpet was layered in sh❊t. Perfect.

Hartman was so mortified that I took pity and stopped myself from strangling him. He wanted to start cleaning it up—but he didn't know what to do first. I knew what I had to do. Ten pounds of poop, a roll of paper towels, and a bottle of alcohol later (no, not to drink—although a shot just about then would have helped), my carpet was as good as new.

I tell this story for two reasons: (1) The rubbing-alcohol cleaning fix I describe in this section really works great. No poop smell, no stain, no kidding! And (2) if you ever drop in at my place, shoes come off at the door.

CARPET FIXES

Here's the thing about fixing a damaged, stained, or burned carpet: The results might not be as seamless as you'd hoped. The thing to remember, though, is that although the fix may not be perfect, it should leave your carpet looking better than it did with the damage.

The best way to keep a carpet looking like new is to vacuum regularly. Built-up soil, walked over day after day, breaks down the carpet fibers and makes it age prematurely.

Fixing Surface Damage

If your carpet has a surface burn or stain, use a pair of scissors to trim away the damage. Hold the scissors horizontally and start to shear in small snips until the marred area is cut away. Don't cut deeper than you have to—it's like going too short with a haircut, except carpet won't grow back!

Fixing Deep Damage

Use this fix if your carpet is damaged down to the padding. One thing to consider is that a carpet patch may not match the color of your existing carpet, since colors usually fade and discolor over time. But remember, as long as the fix looks better than the damage, you'll be in good shape.

TOOLS
- Utility knife
- Piece of scrap carpet (a few inches larger than your damaged area)
- Pencil
- Paintbrush (for applying glue)
- Carpet glue
- Books or weights
- Old hairbrush or comb

1. With a utility knife, cut out the damaged section in the shape of a triangle (a three-sided cutout patches better than a four-sided one).
2. Take the cutout and place it over the back of a scrap piece of carpet. (If you don't have scrap, cut a piece from an obscure part of the carpet, like inside a closet or under an armoire.) Because carpets have a "grain" (some have patterns as well), be sure the grain of your patch matches that of your cutout. To check the grain,

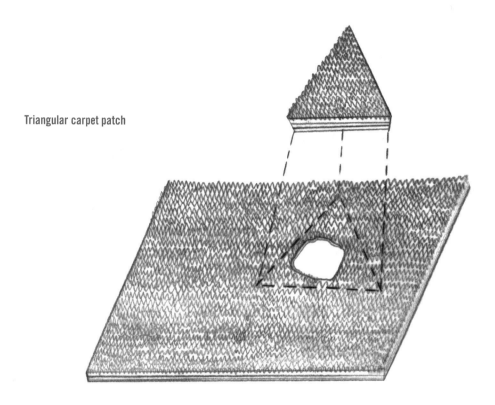

Triangular carpet patch

brush your hand over the carpet fibers in one direction to see which way the grain goes.

3. Once you have the cutout properly aligned, trace it over the back of the scrap with a pencil.
4. Cut out the patch with the utility knife.
5. Brush carpet glue around the seams of the cutout section of your carpet.
6. Position and drop in the patch—pressing around the seams.
7. Place a few heavy books or weights over the patch and let it dry overnight.
8. With an old hairbrush or comb, feather out the patch fibers into the

existing carpet.

Spot Cleaning a Stain

Rubbing alcohol is a great spot cleaner. First test for colorfastness in an inconspicuous corner. If the carpet color doesn't fade, use a paper towel to absorb and/or lift up any surface soil. Then pour enough alcohol over the stain to saturate it and wipe with a rag. Repeat as necessary. Once the soil is scrubbed away, press a paper towel over the spot to absorb excess alcohol. The alcohol cleanses, deodorizes, then evaporates—not leaving any soapy residue in the carpet, which is a good thing.

Windows
and Doors

WINDOWS AND DOORS BASIX: OPEN OPPORTUNITIES FOR MAKING YOUR HOME SAFE AND SOUND

They say the eyes are the windows of the soul. (If that's true, how come I once fell for a guy with smoldering brown eyes and a soul as rotten as the day is long? I guess appearances can be deceiving, both in buildings and boyfriends—but that's a subject for a different book.) Well, your windows and doors are the eyes of your house. They open up to beautiful views, they welcome guests, they bring light to darkness, and they shut tight when we need to protect ourselves. So if it's unsticking a window or installing a peephole, the following fixes will be nothing less than eye-opening.

Whether they're floor to ceiling with an ocean view or single-hung overlooking an alley, every home has windows. No matter what their shape or size, other than being a porthole, windows need to provide two basic functions—insulation and security—and that's exactly what will be covered in this section. As for the view, you're on your own.

WINDOW SAFETY

More than 15,000 children in the United States fall from windows each year. A horrifying statistic, especially when it's so completely preventable. Window pins are great barriers that not only keep intruders from coming in but also keep children from falling out. Even better from a safety perspective are window guards—they allow the window to be completely opened while blocking a child from climbing out. They keep pets safe, too. But note that window guards are not designed to keep out intruders.

Installing a Window Guard

Window guards come in different sizes and are designed for different types of windows, so make sure you take your window's measurements and know what type you have before purchasing. Their installations vary slightly from brand to brand, but the following is a good general step-by-step for a single- or double-hung window mounted from the interior.

If your windows open larger than the guard, you must install window stops. *Do not allow a gap of more than 4 inches.* Follow window-stop instructions provided by the manufacturer.

TOOLS
- Interior-mounted window-guard kit
- Nail set
- Hammer
- Phillips screwdriver
- Window stops (for windows that open larger than guard permits)

1. Assemble the telescoping grid to the side posts (the grid is retractable, like a curtain rod).

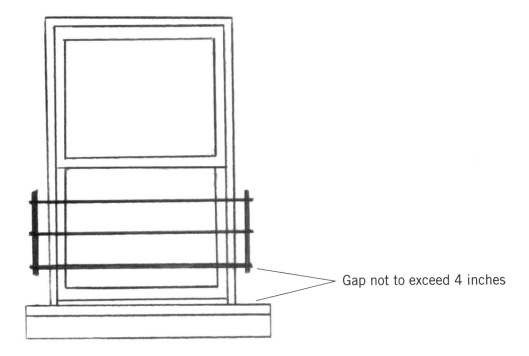

Gap not to exceed 4 inches

2. With the window open, position the entire assembly in your window frame. Be sure to set the side posts far enough back in the frame to allow the window to open and close freely. If your window opens higher than the height of the guard, be sure that the open gap of the window above the guard is not greater than 4 inches. If the gap is larger than 4 inches, purchase window stops that will block the window from exceeding the required size opening allowed for safety.

3. With the guard in place, use the nail set and hammer to make a starter hole where the top corner hole of one side post meets the frame. Drive in the first screw.

4. Level the guard by eye and then make a starter hole on the opposite side of the window for the other side of the guard post. Drive in the second screw by first tapping starter holes with the nail set and hammer and then driving in the screw.

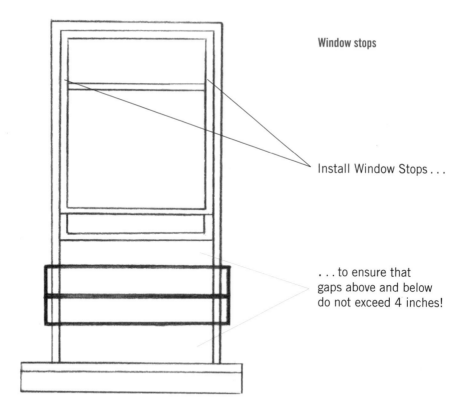

Window stops

Install Window Stops . . .

. . . to ensure that
gaps above and below
do not exceed 4 inches!

5. Once the guard is screwed in place, check that the quick-release
buttons function properly.

Chix Chat:
A Personal Story About Why Window Guards Are a Must

Cousin Sue had just moved to Texas. One day her new neighbor came running up to her house and started pounding on the door in hysterics. She finally managed to blurt out, "Your son! He's on the roof!" Sue tore-ass up the stairs and found the screen pulled out of her two-year-old's bedroom window. There was James, crawling on the roof of their porch, over fifteen feet in the air! The drop from there—concrete driveway.

Sue fought back her panic. In total control, she coached him to lie flat on his belly and crawl back to the window, where she pulled him into the house. As soon as he was safe, she profusely thanked and blessed her neighbor, then went completely numb. She said she was physically sick for over a day at the thought of how narrowly her baby had escaped potential death.

(As a side note, people always ask me how I got started in TV. It's because of my cousin Sue! She used to get such a kick out of the stories I would tell her about my days on the job with Sal. One day she said, "Norma, you should host your own home-improvement show! You would be perfect. You'd bring to home-improvement shows what Emeril brought to cooking shows!" That's just what she said. And I thought . . . *She's nuts.*

Now, I've heard of those "lightbulb moments" that Oprah and Dr. Phil speak about. The day after Cousin Sue said that, a whole Broadway marquee of lightbulbs went BANG on the top of my head. I thought, *Wait a minute, I* could *do a TV show.* And at that exact moment, *Chix Can Fix* was born. Two TV shows, a radio show, and book later, here I am. Thanks, cuz!)

Chix Safety Tips: Finding the Best Window Guard

There are many window guards available today. When buying one, be sure to choose a model that contains the proper safety features. Your window guard should:

- have quick-release buttons in case of emergency
- have spacing between bars that does not exceed 4 inches
- conform to local fire and building codes
- be able to withstand 150 pounds of pressure in its locked position

Installing Security Pins

Here's a great project that will let you sleep better at night. A security pin for your window does two things: It adds a steel-bolt obstruction that will prevent a window from being pried open, plus it allows the window to be secured in small opened positions that will let air into your home, while keeping out intruders. I also like this type of security device because it doesn't require a key—in case there's a fire and you need to escape from a window fast.

Hardware stores and home centers carry an array of these window security devices. They are all relatively easy to install, and the principle is always the same: When the pin is engaged, it slides through the frame of the window and bolts it in place. Just be sure to choose the right push pin for your window type. The following fix uses a common type of security pin that works on sliding windows.

TOOLS

- Push-pin window lock
- Masking tape
- Pencil
- Nail set
- Hammer
- Drill and drill bits
- Safety glasses
- Phillips screwdriver

1. Close and lock your window.
2. The push pin can go on either the top or the bottom of the window—your choice. Once you decide, place a piece of masking tape on the inside corner of the window frame and line up the push-pin lock. (Masking tape will help prevent splintering.)
3. Use a pencil to mark the point where the pin makes contact with the frame.

Chix Tricks: Worry-Free Window Cracking

If you want to install a security pin but still be able to have the window cracked open for ventilation, here's what you do:

1. Pull the window open, but not more than a few inches—you don't want an arm to be able to reach in and pull the pin!
2. Follow steps 3–10 above.

Pin drilling depth

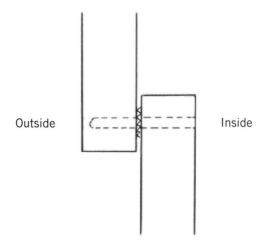

Outside

Inside

Do not allow the drill bit to penetrate
the outer surface of the window.

4. With the nail set and hammer, make a dimple for the drill bit on the marked spot. (This indentation will stop the drill bit from "walking" as you start to drill.)

5. Load the drill with the appropriate drill bit (see the packaged instructions for your pin). If you are drilling into a metal frame instead of wood, you will make this hole in increments—first drill a smaller starter hole and then come back with the pin-size drill bit for the final pass.

6. Put on your safety glasses before you start drilling. Hold the drill steady so that the bit enters *straight* into the frame. Begin drilling. Do not drill all the way through the frame to the exterior—this jeopardizes security. (For single- or double-hung windows, you will go through both frames, but again do not drill through to the exterior.) Clean out any debris from the hole.

7. With the hole made, place the pin into the hole in its proper orientation.

8. Use the pencil to mark the holes for the screws.

9. On these marks make small pilot holes with the smaller drill bit.

10. Drive the fastening screws into these holes (they will be provided with the lock).

CAULKING, GLAZING, AND SEALING WINDOWS

Leaks around windows can be a real pane. (Get it? "Pane"? Come on, it was cute!) What's not cute, however, is that leaks can also lead to real damage to your home. Water that makes it all the way inside can be mopped up, but water that seeps down into the wall will stay there and lead to mold and rot.

It's imperative to determine what is causing the leak. It may appear that the window is leaking, when in fact there is a roof problem or a fault in the siding higher up. Water can run down rafters and joists and cause drips far away from the actual source of the trouble. If this proves to be the case, you may need to call in a contractor for repairs.

Caulking

If you determine that your window is the culprit of the leak in your home, take a close look at the exterior casing and its caulk. Are there any obvious gaps or spots missing caulk? Are there separations in the wood? All of these are places where water can sneak in! If the caulk is missing or damaged, you can easily restore it. Caulk can also be used to seal holes and gaps where the wood has split, as long as the wood is still sound.

Running a bead of caulk

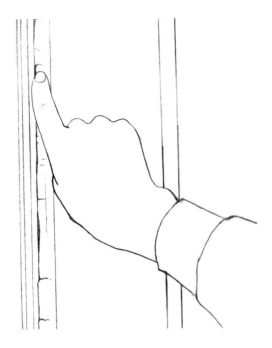

Make sure you buy a caulk that resists mildew, and is waterproof and for exterior use. Caulks are available in water-based or silicone. Some pros say pure silicone caulking may be more resistant than water-based, but I have to let you know that it is way more difficult to work with—it doesn't clean up with water, only a solvent such as mineral spirits. Also, if you intend to paint the area, make sure that the caulk will accept paint.

TOOLS
- Razor scraper
- Disinfectant cleanser or a solution of water and bleach
- Water-based or silicone exterior window caulking
- Utility knife
- Wire hanger
- Caulking gun
- Paper towels
- Rag
- Water or baby oil, as appropriate

1. With a razor scraper, scrape out the old caulking, being sure to hold the scraper at an angle so you don't scratch the paint and wood. Wipe down the window frame and clean with disinfectant cleanser or water/bleach solution.
2. If the joint seems damp (it may smell musty), you must let it dry before applying the caulking.
3. Cut the tip of the caulking tube with a utility knife at an angle. Don't cut off too much of the tip, because the bead will squeeze out too fat. Some brands actually have a guide on the tip that indicates bead thickness.

4. Pierce the seal in the caulking tube with a wire hanger, load the gun, push the plunger forward, and begin squeezing the trigger, which will pump the caulking to the tip.

5. Run a thin bead of caulking along the joint where the window casing meets the siding and then smooth it down by gliding your finger along the length of the joint. Wipe the excess off your finger on a paper towel as you work. Be sure to release the plunger while you're not using the gun so the caulking doesn't continue to ooze out! Keep your finger moist with water or baby oil (if using silicone) to help smooth out the caulking.

6. Let the caulk dry for a day, then paint the area if desired.

Glazing

What if your window is leaking around one of the panes of glass or, worse yet, the glass is loose? No problem, the fix is easy. If you look at the panes, you will see that they are held into the frame with small metal fasteners called glazier's points and are sealed with what looks like caulk. It isn't caulk, though. This material is called glazing, and though it performs a similar function to caulk, it is different to work with. You'll find glazing on older windowpanes. Glazing often dries out and cracks over time, breaking the seal it provides between the glass and frame and causing your window to leak. Although this glazing is no longer used on today's manufactured windows, glazing compound is still available in hardware stores for repairs on older windows.

TOOLS
- Glazier's points
- Pliers (if applicable)
- Glazing compound (no, not for doughnuts, for windows)
- Putty knife
- Water

1. If the glass is falling out of the frame, you must reset it. With the glass held firmly in place, squeeze two to three glazier's points per

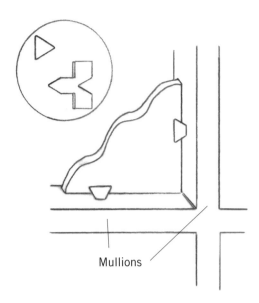

Typical glazer's points; triangular style shown,
installed and ready for glazing

side into the mullion, the piece of wood that divides the window. Position the points so they are evenly spaced. You may need to use a pair of pliers for this step.

2. Open the can of glazing compound, scoop out a small handful, and roll it between your palms like Play-Doh until it is a long, thin snake.

3. Starting in one corner, press the glazing in around the window perimeter with your fingertips. Look at the adjacent panes for an idea of how much to use. Make sure that it is well seated all the way around.

4. Dip a putty knife in water and then use it to smooth the glazing around the perimeter of the window. Go slowly—it can be like working with cake icing that is too dry. If you planned on painting, glazing can be painted as soon as it goes on.

Putty knife smoothing

Sealing with Weather Stripping

Even if your windows don't leak, they may be costing you money by letting cold air in and warm air out (vice versa in the summer). It is common for older windows to seat improperly, causing gaps and drafts. Fortunately, there are a variety of commercially available weatherstripping products. They come in different thicknesses, colors, and materials. Foam is cheaper, but vinyl is more durable. Choose the one that best suits your needs.

Weather stripping is easy to install. It comes in a long coil with adhesive already applied. Depending on the window, it may be visible once installed, but it shouldn't be that unsightly, especially if the color is similar to the window frame's. The bottom line is that the part of the window that moves has to be sealed against the part that is fixed. Unless the gap is huge, stripping should be required only on one side. Although this material is primarily for fixing drafts, it can stop leaks that are caused by gusting rain, too.

TOOLS

- Roll of weather stripping
- Scissors or a utility knife

1. Roll out a length of stripping that is slightly longer than the length of one side of your window. On a double-hung window (window panels that move vertically), the stripping would go on the bottom edge of the window, the part that comes in contact with the jamb. On a sliding window (a window that moves horizontally), the stripping would go on the vertical edge.
2. With scissors or a utility knife, cut your pieces.
3. Peel a few inches of backing from one end of the stripping. Begin applying it to the window, not to the jamb, starting from one side and working your way across the edge. Peel the backing and press the stripping in place as you go.

UNSTICKING WINDOWS

Before you get a hernia trying to pull open a stuck window, make sure that it hasn't been nailed closed by the past dweller. Once you're sure it can be opened, it's time to get out the utility knife. Most windows won't open because they've been painted shut. Lazy, bad painters! The problem could also be due to sticky or too narrow window channels (the U-shaped frame around the window).

Remember: You will be working next to glass, so be careful not to get overzealous with your scraping and don't break the pane.

Chix Tricks: Painted Window Perfection

When painting windows, you should work with a practically dry brush where the sashes meet the channels. Also, you should raise and lower the windows while they are drying so the paint never gets the chance to stick where it's not supposed to.

Opening Windows That Are Painted Shut

TOOLS
- Utility knife
- Block of wood
- Hammer
- Scraper

1. At a sharp angle, run the utility knife where the sash (the framework that holds the pane) meets the sash groove (aka window channel). Work gently—it's the paint you're going after, not the frame.
2. Hold the block of wood against the sash of the window and lightly tap with the hammer in the direction the window needs to move in order to open. This should do the trick.
3. Once the window is open, pass the scraper up and down the sashes to scrape off the built-up paint.

Lubricating Window Channels

TOOLS
- Graphite spray lubricant

If paint doesn't seem to be the problem, you'll want to work on the window channels (sash groove). Spray them down with graphite lubricant. I specify graphite because it's known as a "dry" spray—it's greaseless and won't pick up dust or grit, which would exacerbate the sticking.

Widening Window Channels

TOOLS
- Block of wood (twice the length of your hand)
- Hammer

If swelling seems to be the problem, you can try to widen the channels. Place the block of wood in the channel lengthwise and tap it with the hammer. Continue this process the length of each channel.

Chix Chat:
How I Almost Killed the Pizza Guy

I was tired of hearing my friend Joey complain about how he couldn't see out the front door when visitors came to his home. If he wasn't expecting a pizza, he'd let the knocking go on and on like a bad percussion solo, until the unknown caller got tired and went away. Now, this was a guy who could pick up a pair of sticks and play the drums like a god. But when it came to picking up a screwdriver, the man was lost. I called him one day to tell him I had a surprise for him—I had to let him know I was coming, because if I just showed up unannounced, *I'd* be the unknown caller soloing on his front door.

I arrive at his place wearing work boots, gloves, and safety glasses and carrying my drill and toolbox—I was on a mission. I don't know if he was in shock at my appearance or thought it better not to question a woman carrying a drill, but he didn't say a word—he simply let me go ahead and do my thing.

Just as I was about to bore a hole through his front door, there was a knock. Annoyed that I was being interrupted in the midst of my drilling rapture, I swung the door open and blurted out a nasty, *"Can I help you?"* The pizza guy's eyeballs nearly popped out of his head. Now, I knew I was being a little rude, but what hadn't dawned on me was that I was standing there pointing a loaded drill at him, wearing crazy commando goggles, and looking like a deranged serial killer. Good thing Joey came over, laughing hysterically at the scene he'd just walked in on. I apologized profusely, and a few laughs (and a big tip) later, Joey and I shared a pizza and admired his brand-new peephole.

The truth is that it's dangerous to open your door without seeing who's out there—especially for women living on their own. So if you don't have a way to see who's at your door, you must install a peephole.

Drilling a peephole with a hole saw

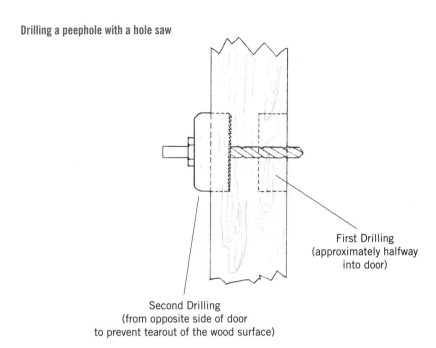

First Drilling
(approximately halfway
into door)

Second Drilling
(from opposite side of door
to prevent tearout of the wood surface)

DOORS

Installing a Peephole

When purchasing a peephole, there are a couple of things to consider besides size, style, and finish. Pay attention to the following:

- Field of view: This measures how many degrees you can see out the peephole. Older styles let you see only the head of the person on the other side of the door, not protecting you from someone who could be hiding by squatting down beneath eye level. I suggest a field of view of approximately 180 degrees.
- Distance for viewability: This indicates how close you need to be to the peephole to look out the door. Today there are brands that feature seven-foot viewability—that means a child or person in a wheelchair could see out the viewer without having to put his or her eye up against it.
- One-way view: This assures that you can see clearly out but nobody on the outside can see in—at all.

This project can be used to install a peephole in a wooden or a metal door. Just be sure to use bits in your drill that are suited for the type of door you have—specifications are listed on the packaging for your bit.

TOOLS
- Tape measure
- Pencil
- Nail punch
- Hammer
- Newspaper
- Safety glasses
- Dust mask
- Drill and small drill bit
- Hole saw or spade bit (see installation instructions for recommended bit and size)
- Peephole
- Large flathead screwdriver

1. With the tape measure, find the center point on your door. Then find a comfortable height for the peephole and mark it with a pencil. At that point make a starter hole with the nail punch and hammer.
2. Place the newspaper under the door and put on your safety glasses and dust mask.
3. Load a drill with the small drill bit to make a pilot hole. Hold the drill level and drill straight through the door. (See "Your Power Drill Is Your Friend," page 136.)
4. Load your drill with the recommended hole-cutting bit. With your pilot hole as your guide, start drilling the hole. Be sure to hold the drill straight. Cut only halfway through the door (this will avoid "blowout"—splintering on the other side of the door).
5. Close the door and, with the pilot hole as your guide, cut through the other side, again, being sure to hold the drill straight.
6. Clean away any debris.
7. The two sides of the peephole viewer usually come screwed together. Unscrew the unit and fit the viewing lens on the inside of the door, then fit the other piece from the outside of the door. They'll

screw together to the appropriate door width. Screw them until they're snug, and then further tighten by placing a screwdriver in the slots on the housing of the viewing lens.

Installing a Door Sweep

Those little Scottie dog–shaped draft stoppers that you find in country-chic gift shops are certainly one effective way to block drafts . . . until you want to open your door. Then they just get in your way and, in my house, end up being tossed into a corner and eventually into the garbage (or are passed along to the next victim as a recycled Secret Santa gift). There's a better way to keep out door drafts!

There are various types of door sweeps, ranging in price and style. They may be made of vinyl or metal. Some mount to the exterior face of the door, others to the interior. Some rise up when they are being opened and drop when the door is closed—this type may be a good option if you have thick carpeting or a rug where the door opens. Check them all out and see which you like best for your situation. Just make sure you buy one wide enough for your door! Wider is fine, because they will be cut. Always read installation instructions provided with the packaging.

TOOLS
- Tape measure
- New door sweep
- Fine-tooth hacksaw
- Utility knife
- Sandpaper or file (if the sweep is metal)
- Pencil
- Nail set
- Hammer
- Drill and drill bit (size depends on door-sweep instructions)
- Safety glasses
- Phillips screwdriver

1. With a tape measure, measure the width of your door. Be sure to buy a door sweep wide enough to cover your door. Before cutting, read the instructions to determine accurate door-sweep length—

they will probably direct you to subtract a specified amount for proper fit.

2. Take that measurement and mark it on the door sweep.

3. Cut the sweep with the hacksaw. If it has separate pieces that come apart, cut each one individually. The vinyl or brush seal may cut more easily with a utility knife.

4. Sand or file down the cut end.

5. With the door closed, position the sweep and mark the screw holes with the pencil. Set the sweep aside.

6. Punch the marks with the nail set and hammer.

7. Load the drill with the appropriate drill bit and, with your safety glasses on, drill the holes for the screws. Drill only as deep as the screws are long—don't drill through the door! (See "Your Power Drill Is Your Friend," page 136.)

8. Position the sweep and set the screws with the screwdriver, but do not tighten them completely.

9. Open and close the door to check the sweep height. The sweep should be in good contact with the door but not interfere with the door's movement.

10. Make your adjustments and tighten down the screws.

Replacing a Doorknob

Whether you're replacing the knob of the bathroom door, the closet door, or the front door, the installation is the same. Doorknobs come in two halves that slide together through a hole in the door, are interlocked through a locking mechanism, and then are screwed together by two long machine screws.

TOOLS
- Phillips screwdriver
- New doorknob set

TO REMOVE THE OLD DOORKNOB AND LOCKING MECHANISM

1. Unscrew the two screws found around the base of the knob.

2. Pull the handle halves apart and out of the door.

3. To remove the locking mechanism, locate the two screws holding the latch in place. Once they're out, you'll be able to pull out the entire locking mechanism.

TO INSTALL THE NEW DOORKNOB SET

1. Refer to the installation instructions to identify all the parts and their proper placement.

2. Insert the locking mechanism, being sure that the latch is in its correct orientation. Screw it in place.

3. Line up the doorknobs, making sure that the long prong of the locking mechanism enters properly into the knob. Verify that you're putting the right knob on the right side of the door!

4. Install the long machine screws into the base of the knob. Be patient, because it may take time to catch the threads and then, because the screws are so long, it will take a moment to screw them all the way in.

5. Check that the set locks properly. If not, take it apart. Look at the instructions, since you may need to readjust the locking mechanism.

And just like that, you have yourself a new doorknob!

Installing a Dead Bolt

No matter how safe your neighborhood is, it just makes sense to have a secure lock. I recommend buying a lock-installation kit. It will contain a $2\frac{1}{8}$-inch-diameter hole saw, a $\frac{7}{8}$-inch hole saw or spade bit, and a handy drilling jig that takes the guesswork out of the placement of the holes in the door. You can get one of these kits at most hardware stores or home centers. If you choose to install your dead bolt sans kit, you will still need to purchase (or borrow) the hole saw and bits separately.

TOOLS
- Pencil
- Tape measure
- Tape
- Lock-installation kit (which includes a $2\frac{1}{8}$-inch hole saw and a

$\frac{7}{8}$-inch spade bit) or a hole saw and spade bit in sizes required by the lock manufacturer's installation instructions

- Speed square
- Drill
- Newspaper
- Safety glasses
- Chisel
- Screwdriver

1. Make a pencil mark at the height you want the dead bolt. The height of most doorknobs is about 36 inches from the floor, and dead bolts are typically installed 4 to 6 inches above the knob.
2. Tape the template provided with the lock set, or clamp the jig that comes with your installation kit onto the door to establish exactly where the dead bolt holes will be made. Check your measurements and positioning carefully before drilling (read the instructions). If the holes end up in the wrong place, your dead bolt simply won't work and you'll have big ol' "oops" holes in your door—not a good thing.

Drilling dead bolt with a hole slaw

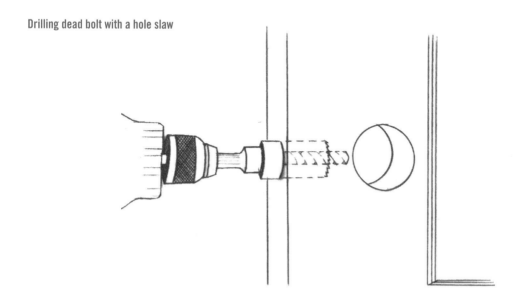

3. Using the speed square, transfer a line from the center of the lock hole to the edge of the door for the bolt hole. The bolt hole will be drilled on this line, centered on the door. You should be aware that all doors are not the same thickness. Exterior doors are thicker, usually $1\frac{3}{4}$ inches, while interior doors are only $1\frac{3}{8}$ inches thick. Make sure to double-check. Once you have your layout marked, it's time to drill.

4. With the door closed, newspaper slid under it to protect the floor, and your safety glasses on, load the drill with the hole saw and start drilling the lock hole, being sure to hold the drill straight and steady. (See "Your Power Drill Is Your Friend, page 136.) When using a hole saw, you must be careful to have a good grip on the drill. A drill with an accessory handle is best, and be sure to use a slower speed when cutting.

    Do not drill all the way through; drill only until the pilot bit appears on the other side—this will prevent splintering or "blowout," which occurs when a bit comes through the back side of a hole. At that point move the drill to the other side of the door and complete the hole.

5. Change to the smaller bit and drill the bolt hole from the edge of the door perpendicular to the lock hole. Again hold the drill straight and steady.

6. Once the necessary holes are drilled, the edge of the door must be mortised (chiseled) to receive the bolt faceplate. Slide the bolt into the hole as far as it will go and, with a pencil, trace the outline onto the door. Make sure that it is square when you do this. The outline marks the area that has to be mortised so that the faceplate and bolt will set in nice and flush. It's a little tedious, but it has to be done, or the lock won't fit and the door won't close. Chisel carefully and test the depth often by inserting the bolt—you want the surface of the faceplate to be flush with the door edge.

> ## Chix Tip: Depth Perception— How to Dodge Drilling Too Deep
>
> Instead of guessing how deep is too deep, wrap a piece of masking tape around your drill bit at the desired depth. Now when you're drilling, you'll know to stop when the tape reaches the material you're drilling into.

7. Slide the bolt into position, making sure that it's right side up (check the instructions).

8. Slide the left and right halves of the lock into position. The installation details differ from lock to lock, so review the diagram that comes with yours. When you have them positioned correctly, you will not have to force them. Make sure that the side with the screw holes faces the inside. The lock won't do much good if it can be unscrewed from the outside!

9. Fasten the halves together with a screwdriver, but leave them a little loose for the moment.

10. Screw down the bolt faceplate. Once this is done, you can snug together the screws holding the lock.

11. The only thing left to do is to install the strike plate on the doorjamb. This must be aligned carefully with the bolt to ensure smooth operation of the lock. Use the $\frac{7}{8}$-inch spade bit to drill a receiver hole deep enough to allow the dead bolt to extend fully. Usually there is a pair of extra-long screws provided for securing this plate. They are designed to penetrate into the studs behind the doorframe to make the lock even more secure. Once the strike plate is mortised and installed, your dead bolt installation is done! (If the dead bolt doesn't close smoothly because of a misaligned strike plate, see "Adjusting a Strike Plate," below).

Adjusting a Strike Plate

If you have to jiggle your door to actually lock it, it means the latch or bolt isn't properly positioning in the hole of the strike plate. But here's a great chix fix for it!

TOOLS
- Scotch tape
- Lipstick
- Phillips screwdriver
- Small wood chisel
- Hammer

1. Cover the strike plate with a piece of Scotch tape.

2. Apply lipstick to the tip of the bolt or latch — use that ugly shade the fashion magazines were trying to convince us was the new red.

3. For latch alignment, close the door while holding the knob so the latch is retracted. For bolt alignment, just close the door.

4. Now release the latch or turn the bolt so the lipstick marks the Scotch tape — do this repeatedly so the lipstick leaves a clear mark.

5. Open the door and check where the lipstick made its mark — that's where the strike plate should be adjusted to! See if it has to be raised, lowered, moved to the right or left — make a mental note.

6. Remove the tape and then unscrew the mounting screws of the plate.

7. With the chisel and hammer, chisel out the area of the doorframe that the strike plate needs to be repositioned to — this shouldn't require much chiseling. It's better to do a little at a time than to chisel out too much.

8. Remount the plate and test the latch or bolt. If it's still sticky, repeat steps 1–7 — make sure you're chiseling in the right place!

> ## Chix Tip: Strike Plate Savvy
>
> When installing a new doorknob, it really isn't necessary that you replace the strike plate. But if your new doorknob has a different finish and you want to match them, just unscrew the two screws found at the top and the bottom of the plate and replace it with the one that comes with the doorknob set.

Unsticking a Door

One of the most common and frustrating problems with doors is when they stick or rub against the jamb or floor. You might blame the carpenter for doing a sloppy job when the door was installed, but chances are it's not her fault!

Most doors are made of wood, which is susceptible to changes in humidity (hygroscopic behavior). Low humidity makes wood shrink, while moist air causes swelling. Since doors are fitted with a fairly small gap, usually about $\frac{1}{8}$ inch, it doesn't take much moisture to make a door expand and rub against the jamb.

Another reason your door might stick is sagging. If its hinges don't adequately support its weight, a door that started out square and plumb can start to sag. This happens frequently with interior doors that stand open most of the time. Also, the jamb itself may become out of square due to settling of the house.

Regardless of why your door sticks, the solution is the same. You have to remove some wood from the edge at the spot where the door sticks.

TOOLS
- Pencil
- Nail set and hammer (for door removal, if applicable)
- Safety glasses
- Newspaper
- Block plane
- Medium-grit sandpaper

1. It goes without saying (but I'll say it anyway) that if the door is wet from a leak, fix the leak and let it dry out. This may take awhile, and the door probably will never return to its original size, but it will help.
2. Close the door and visually inspect where it is rubbing. This may be obvious if paint is missing in spots. Make light pencil marks to show where it is touching. If the door is rubbing at the floor, you'll need to take it off the hinges to work on it (just pop out the hinges with a nail set and hammer).
3. Put on your safety glasses and line the floor beneath the door with newspaper. Start by removing a little wood with the plane. Use long strokes, taking a thin shaving off on each pass.
4. Keep testing the door fit while you're working to see how it's going. If the door is sticking badly, you may wind up removing quite a bit of stock, but that's okay.

5. Once the door closes smoothly, take off just a little more to compensate for paint thickness if you're going to paint the door. If you do paint, make sure the paint is completely dry before you close the door!

6. The plane will leave sharp edges on its cuts, so use some medium-grit sandpaper to smooth them down.

Conclusion

What Chix Can Fix *Is Really All About*

Sometimes people ask me who I work for. My answer, *Chix Can Fix*—without fail, they giggle. Then I say, *"No, I'm serious, Chix Can Fix is my corporation, it's the title of my book, it's my philosophy of life!"* That's when the reaction changes from *Yuck, yuck,* to *Oh, this girl means business.* Women become intrigued and excited. Men, on the other hand, have varied reactions.

For the most part, the vast majority of men totally dig it. For them, the idea of women taking charge of the responsibilities that gender bias has put on them for centuries is a huge relief. Plus, they think it's sexy. Women and power tools—oh yeah, that's *hot.*

Then there are the others . . .

I once had a guy say to me, "Oh, so you're one of them modern broads, trying to be all free and sh*t." Of course I busted out laughing, because he was certainly joking—or was he? Could it be that we women who are self-reliant and strong somehow make those men feel unneeded and weak? Or is it that our independence gives them less control over us? If my ability to use a circular saw is a blow to his ego, then guess what? He's a loser. Knowing a woman who can sweat pipes should be inspiring, not emasculating.

I remember a guy once telling me to "just let the man be the man." I bit my tongue, folded my hands (so I wouldn't sock him), took a deep breath, and said, "Just because you walk into a bathroom marked MEN doesn't make you a *man*," and walked away. (That's a gem I learned from Aunt Rose-Marie.)

A real man honors and respects independent women. Don't get me wrong—open the door for me, bring me flowers, pick me up, and carry me over a puddle so I don't ruin my brand-new Manolo Blahniks—now *that's* being a man too.

What it all boils down to is this: A woman should not have to rely on anyone, man or woman, to take care of her business and get the job done.

I've learned a lot on my **Chix Can Fix** journey. When I was younger and more naïve, I thought love fixed it all. I still believe love is the answer to the age-old question *What is life really all about?* But let's face it, in the world we live in today, "All you need is love" doesn't pay the rent, secure a job, or fix the plumbing.

Although written with love, this book has given you another powerful *L* word—*leverage*—not only to change a light switch and repair your plumbing, but to realize that you can take control of your reality and be self-reliant and powerful.

Chix Can Fix is about being totally in the dark about something, even frightened by it, and going for it anyway. I've learned that by doing this you can walk through your life with more poise and confidence. You take that sense of accomplishment with you everywhere you go. Suddenlyyou're no longer the victim, the helpless girl—now that's leverage!

You have leverage to negotiate that position in your company, chase that lifelong dream, get out of that toxic relationship, help that person in need. That leverage enables you to take down the walls that confine you, open up windows of opportunity, and rewire your negative thought patterns. It's that very leverage that builds the ultimate sense of empowerment—loving yourself. And that's *Chix Can Fix*.

Appendix

Tool Basix

The adage *"You get what you pay for"* usually applies when you're purchasing tools. I know you may be inclined to buy an inexpensive tool, thinking, "Hey, I just need it for this one project." Wrong. Once you get started fixing, you'll find you're reaching for tools over and over again. Cheap tools often don't perform properly— the head strips, the plastic cracks—and you end up thoroughly frustrated with a tool that's not getting the job done. And that can suck all the fun out of your project!

It just makes sense to buy a good quality tool from the jump. Go for brands with warranties, check out what the pros load in their tool belt, ask home-improvement aficionados their opinion, etc. I also recommend buying the tools you'll need for the specific project you're going to tackle. With each new project your tool collection will grow—along with your skills!

Getting the right tool the first time around will in the long run save you time, money, and frustration—now that's priceless.

TOOLS LIST

The following is a list of every tool you'll need for the fixes in this book and then some. It's also a great reference guide to stock a killer tool box!

General Tools

Adjustable wrench (aka crescent)

Needle-nose or long-nose pliers

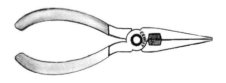

Slip-joint or adjustable pliers

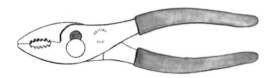

Flathead or slotted screwdriver

Tongue-and-groove pliers
(aka Channellocks)

Phillips screwdriver

Allen wrenches

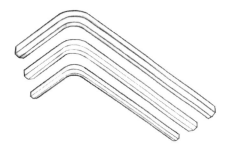

Nail set

Star Drive (Torx)

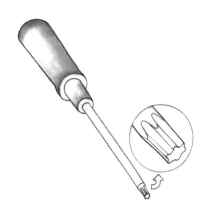

Hacksaw

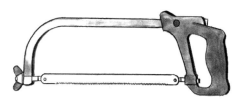

Hammer

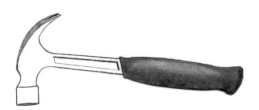

Hand saw

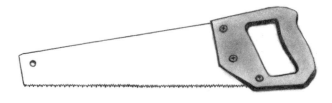

Rubber mallet

Block plane

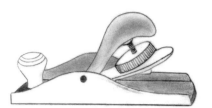

Scraper

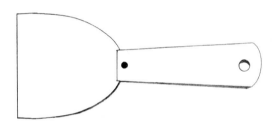

Tape measure

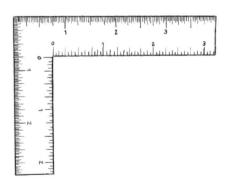

Wood chisel

Square

Utility knife

Cordless drill

Razor scraper

Wood bits

Masonry bit

Paddle or spade bit

Hole saw bit

Caulking gun

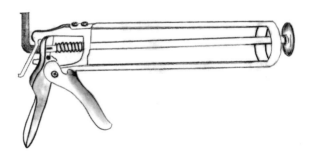

Glue-injecting syringe

Plumbing Specific

Powered plumber's snake

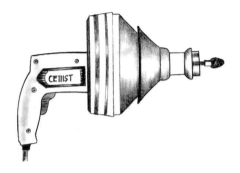

Manual plumber's snake

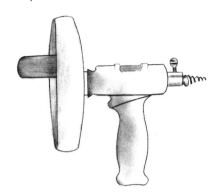

Pipe cutter

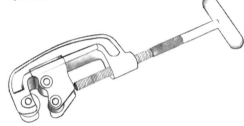

Plumber's tape or Teflon tape

PVC cutters

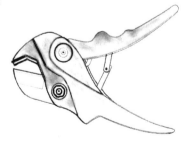

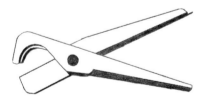

Seat wrench

Seat-dresser tool

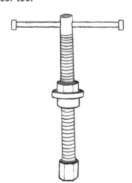

Sink plunger

Toilet plunger

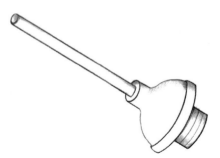

Toilet or closet auger

Electrical Specific

Wire strippers

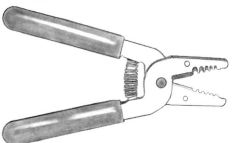

Fuse puller

Multimeter, voltage
or VOM meter

Voltage indicator
(pen type)

Circuit tester
or analyzer

Duct tape

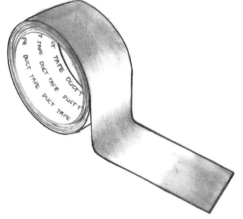

Electrical tape

Drywall/Masonry Specific

Sanding block and pad

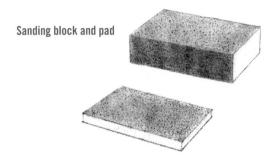

Notched trowel

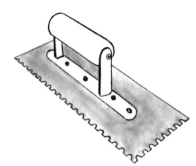

Rubber float

Drywall or jab saw

Masonry chisel

Grout saw

Index

O

Oil hot-water tanks, 73
OOK Hanging Hardware, 149
Organic-matter stains, wall, 147
O-rings, faucet, 45, 53
Outlets, 101–7
    ground fault circuit interrupter
        (GFCI). *See* Ground fault
        circuit interrupter (GFCI)
    replacing, 101–3

P

Patches, drywall. *See* Drywall
Peephole, drilling, 186
    installing, 187–89
Pen stains, wall, 147
Phillips screwdriver, 205
Pilot light, relighting, 70–71
Pipe cutter, 210
Plane, block, 207
Plaster walls, 139–44
    crack and hole repairs, 139
    skim coating, 140–43
Plastic wall anchors, 148
Plug-type fuse replacement, 93–94
Plumber's snake, 63, 210
Plumber's (Teflon) tape, 210
Plumbing, 7–79
    aerators, 39–40
    faucets. *See* Faucets
    hot-water tanks. *See* Hot-water
        tanks
    pop-ups. *See* Pop-ups sink;
        Pop-ups, tub
    shower arm, 41, 43
    showerheads, 39, 40–43
    sinks. *See* Sinks

    toilets. *See* Toilets
    tubs. *See* Tubs
    water heaters. *See* Hot-water tanks
    water system, 11–15
Plungers
    bathroom sinks, 59–60, 211
    toilets, 34–36, 211
Pop-ups, sink
    adjusting, 58
    cleaning, 56
    clevis screw and, 57, 58
    fixing, 56
Pop-ups, tub, 64–65
Power drills, 136–38
P-trap, 12
    removal, 60–61
PVC cutter, 210

R

Razor scraper, 208
Rubber float, 157, 213
Rubber mallet, 207
Rubbing alcohol, as spot cleaner, 169

S

Safety tips
    asbestos, 159
    chemical drain cleaners, 61
    tile, 159
    window guards, 176
Sanding block and pad, 213
Sash groove. *See* Window channels,
    lubricating
Saws
    drywall (jab), 130, 213
    hacksaw, 23, 206

locating, 13–15

shutoff valve. *See* Shutoff valve

Water meter, 12, 14

Water stains, wall, 146

Water-supply lines

flexible, 73–76

toilet, 24, 25–26

Water-supply system, 12

locating and labeling, 13–15

Water system, 11–15

Wax gasket, toilet, 27–29

Weather stripping windows, 183–84

Window channels, lubricating, 185

Window guard installation, 173–75

Windows, 172–85

caulking, 178–81

glazing, 181–83

painted, 185

safety precautions, 172–73, 176

sealing, 183–84

security pins, 176–78

unsticking, 184–85

weather stripping for, 183–84

window channels, lubricating, 185

window guard installation, 173–75

Wire nut/cap, 89–90

Wires, 88–90

cutting, 88

joining, 89

stripping, 88–89

Wire stripper/cutter, 88, 212

Wood chisel, 207

Wrenches

adjustable (crescent), 205

allen, 206

seat, 211

Norma Vally *is a construction pro* with the tools and attitude to get the job done. But this former model and personal trainer is hardly what you would envision when you call for a handyman. For Norma, however, she's just doing what she loves.

As a young girl, born and raised in Brooklyn, Norma worked alongside her father fixing things in their home. Maintenance on the boiler, repairing a leaky faucet, oil changes in the driveway—she was always happy fixing things and finding out how they worked—and she had a knack for it from an early age.

So how did Norma, a woman with degrees in English literature and psychology, find her way back to her true calling? It was a move to a century-old house as an adult that helped Norma learn how to handle home repairs, from wiring and plumbing to demolition and carpentry. She then worked with a general contractor where she would tackle every kind of job on a work site. You can imagine the reaction of fellow workers and customers when she arrived on a construction site in work boots, ready to swing her hammer.

About the Author

Now, as the feisty host of Discovery Home Channel's new series *Toolbelt Diva,* Norma pairs up with female homeowners to tackle a variety of real-life home-improvement projects. *Toolbelt Diva* proves that any woman can take on just about any home-improvement project with the help of Norma's knowledge and confidence. Presented in an informative and nonintimidating way, *Toolbelt Diva* has plenty of information and insight for men as well.

Norma also loves to talk and she does just that as the *Toolbelt Diva* on Discovery Channel Radio, broadcasting nationwide on Sirius Satellite.

Prior to hosting her own TV and radio shows, Norma was the construction pro on Discovery Channel's *Rally Round the House.* She makes appearances on Fox's *Good Day New York,* CNNfn, and talk shows such as *Life & Style, Northwest Afternoon,* and *Tony Danza.* Feeding her other talent and passion, for cooking, Norma has also appeared as a guest on such shows as *Cookin' in Brooklyn.* She is also a sought-after speaker at home shows and expos across the country.

Check out what Norma is up to on www.chixcanfix.com.